Think for Yourself

Think for Yourself

A Memoir

Rupert Metzroth

Fiction Publishing, Inc.
Fort Pierce, Florida

For my wife, Almut,
Our sons, Veit, Riko, and Eitel,
And grandsons,
Erik, Alexander, Richard, Ryan, and John,

And in memory of
My parents, Nikolaus and Christina,
My son, Nicord,
And my brother, Karl

Acknowledgements

In appreciation of the help and encouragement
I received from the Writers Group
at the Morningside Library, Port St. Lucie, Florida,
and the Ft. Pierce Writers Group

Preface

Born in 1926 in Germany, I grew up in a world of divisions.
On the one hand was the peer pressure of my fellow
members of the Hitler Youth and on the other the gentle
persuasion of my father to

"Think for yourself."

On the following pages I describe my efforts
to live by my parents' motto.

My platoon before Anzio. I am second from right.

MY EIGHTEENTH BIRTHDAY,
20 September 1944

Wait, I hear voices outside! They finally came to relieve me and bring me food! Leaning my rifle against the table, I opened the door to greet them.

Oh shit! Facing the whole American army, I slammed the door shut. There must have been at least five or six of them. They had scattered at the sight of me and must have been as scared as I was. Oh, man, what now? There was no back door to escape; and I had only five rounds in my rifle. Because I had left my belt with the bullets in the ammo storage nearby, I had no alternative: Slowly I opened the door, expecting a fusillade of bullets tearing into me. When no shots were fired, I walked, with my hands up, out into the open. Gradually my foes came from behind their cover, six rifles aimed at me. *Damn! What now?*

One guy, short, mean-looking, and with the bayonet on his rifle, moved behind me and poked me forward. I felt the point of the bayonet in my back. *Is that how you die? Without heroics, in total confusion?*

Then, a soldier who seemed to be the leader instructed one of the men to search me. While he frisked me I blurted out, "No arms, I have no arms."

That got the attention of the group. "Hey, the kid speaks English," a tall soldier said. Some of their exchanges I could understand, although they didn't sound the way my high school teacher had taught us.

The little guy still kept poking me with his bayonet. I expected a bullet in my back any second. "Calm down!" the man they called Sarge yelled at him.

"Where did you learn to speak English, kid?" the sergeant asked me.

Why do these people call me a kid? Somehow I remember that a kid is a young goat. Why does he call me a goat?

"I learn in high school."

By now the Americans had relaxed. They surrounded me, observing me with curiosity.

Man, they are just as dirty as I am. Some of them have beards. I'm getting weak from hunger. Must not faint in front of them. The faint feeling subsided and I could concentrate again on my surroundings.

"Hey, kid, how old are you?" *There is that goat again.*

"I am seventeen years old. No, wait, I am eighteen years old. Today is my birthday."

"Your birthday? This is your lucky day. Happy birthday." He grinned. "Are you alone?"

"Yes, I not know where my company is. I must guard ammo in other house."

In the morning, I had rolled off the stacked mortar ammo baskets, the only place to sleep off the floor. My helmet had served as a pillow. The foam insert in the paratrooper helmet was more comfortable than the regular headgear. I stretched to get some of the kinks out of my back and limbs.

The weather was gradually changing to autumn in the Apennini Mountains. I was cold and hungry. A cup of ersatz coffee might have numbed the hunger and warmed me up, no matter how poor its taste. I had eaten the last hunk of *Kommissbrot*, the German army staple, two days earlier. The accompanying sausage with its rotten smell did not tempt me. What a way to celebrate my birthday. I had to find something to eat, perhaps a handful of overripe tomatoes from the nearby field.

Sleeping with my rifle next to me had given me some feeling of safety. One never knew if Italian partisans were around. I had picked up my weapon and left the hovel.

At a house next to a church, a parsonage, a hundred feet down a grassy slope, I hoped to discover something edible. Anything, a raw potato or some corn. The expression, "as poor as a church mouse," applied here, too: nothing but some old books and a rickety table.

Now, the sergeant told one of the others to take me back to a bigger outfit. *What bigger outfit?* My guard looked me over, shouldered his rifle and pointed in the direction he wanted me to go.

This is not happening to me. I'll wake up and it will all be over. Shit, this isn't real.

We stumbled to their headquarters in the rear, following one of those narrow cow paths crossing the mountains. After a while I felt like having a smoke. I turned and asked my guard, "Do you have some paper or maybe newspaper to roll a cigarette? I have tobacco."

We had come to an elevation overlooking a valley. Next to a big boulder he laughed, "Sit down." Joining me, he offered me a cigarette. As we smoked, we observed each other cautiously. He must have been much older than I was, at least twenty-five. On his sleeve he had a patch showing a green pine tree.

"What is your name?" I asked him.

"Herbert Bauer, and yours? How come you speak English?"

"My name is Rupertus Metzroth, and I learn speak English in school. Your name is German? Are you German?"

"No. My grandparents came from Germany a long time ago."

"My great-grandfather come to America in 1850s. In Louisville. He was shoemaker and make shoes for U.S. Army. He went back to Germany, my great-grandmother not want to go to America. I could be American. This is not good, you and me."

"The whole frigging war is not good."

"What is frigging?"

"It's a word we often use in the army," he laughed again.

I added another word to my English vocabulary. I wish I had studied English a little more diligently.

Eventually we arrived at the battalion headquarters. There I noticed four fellow prisoners, but did not know any of them. "Join that group," an MP said.

A short time later I saw my guard, Bauer, slowly leaving the compound. He was obviously reluctant to go back to the front. I hope he made it through the war.

By nightfall a sergeant ordered us into a chicken coop where we made ourselves as comfortable as possible. One of my fellow prisoners asked me whether I was wounded.

"Why?" I asked.

"Because you are bloody in the back."

"Oh, shit. That bum must have stabbed me while he was poking me."

During the night the chicken lice and our lice held a meeting; with their increased activity we did not catch much sleep. *Still no food. What a birthday!*

It occurred to me that my *Soldbuch,* or paybook, contained all sorts of information, such as my various stages of training, including my antiaircraft experience. I did not want my captors to know about the latter, which was recorded in the middle of the sixteen-page booklet. I tore out the four revealing pages, ripped them up, and buried them in the corner under chicken shit.

In the morning we huddled in the front of the coop. A guy in a clean uniform came to collect our paybooks. As he checked them over, he discovered the missing pages.

"Rupertus Metzroth, vortreten," he screamed. I ambled forward; prisoners don't rush.

"That's me," I said in German.

"Where are the missing pages? What do you have to hide?"

"What missing pages?"

"Don't play dumb with me, or I will lead you to the back of the barn and have you shot."

Immediately my fellow prisoners howled, "Leave him alone, you traitor." That action really pissed off the sergeant. He drew his pistol and fired a shot in the air, which put the whole headquarters into turmoil. From all sides, clean soldiers, in contrast to the ones I had encountered at the front, came running with their rifles or pistols. It was a tense situation and I was in the middle of it.

A major appeared, I did not know the rank at the time, only later did I learn the insignia. "What is going on?" he asked.

"Sir, I really do not know what this man wants from me," I said in English with my most innocent kid face.

By now I had turned into a real teen-age rebel, and I did not care what was going to happen to me; too dumb to know my situation.

I had guessed that the guy in the clean uniform was a German. *Probably Bavarian,* I deducted from the slight accent. He must have come to America before the war and was now an intelligence NCO.

My speaking English really set him off, and he was screaming in German something about a spy.

Wide-eyed, I looked at the major and lifted my shoulder, the same gesture we applied when called before the principal. It worked. The major calmed the NCO down and sent the clerks back to their typewriters.

"What is it with this book?" He asked me in English.

"I am a new soldier and that is what the books were like when we came into the Luftwaffe." He bought it and the matter was resolved. But not for my fellow POWs.

"What kind of stunt did you think you could pull with that guy? If you try a number like this again, I'll kick your ass from here to the Alps," one of them said.

He was mad at me but soon calmed down and asked. "Where did you learn to speak English?"

"In high school. I could not let them know that I had been in the service with the antiaircraft for a year. You guys on the front don't know what is going on at home with the bombing and all."

That put me back into their graces.

Soon the major came back. He had in his hand a German rifle grenade, which he tossed leisurely from one hand into the other.

"What is this?" he held the grenade made of Bakelite out for me to see.

I took a step back and said:

"Sir, if you please, this is a German rifle grenade and it is as dangerous for the shooter as it is for the shootee."

He got a funny look on his face and gingerly carried it off.

Our guard had a big grin on his face. I had established rapport with him. We were thirsty, so I asked him for some water.

"I'll be off in half an hour, and then I will bring you some." And he did.

All through my POW time I observed a strange bond between us enlisted Germans and our American guards who were almost sympathetic to the POWs. The feeling among the two sides was nearly unanimous: enlisted men versus officers.

P.O.W. IN ITALY

During the day, more German prisoners of war arrived, among them one from my company. He told me, that due to the gaps between the various German units, the Americans could penetrate our lines. That must have been the case with the group who had taken me prisoner. We had many casualties when the Americans showed up in the rear.

"Was Hubert Müller among them?" I asked.

"No, he disappeared when it was getting hairy."

"Did our guys know that I was taken POW?"

"No, but we knew that you were missing when the runner could not find you two days ago."

Hubert was my buddy dating back to our time at Anzio. He had always taken me under his wing.

On the fourth day without food, I was beginning to get weak. I asked the guard if we could have something to eat.

"You'll be taken back to a prison camp tonight where you'll be fed."

That night, two MPs assembled a strange column: three walking, bandaged GIs led; three mules followed, each with a wounded American on its back; at the end of the line, we prisoners carried a severely wounded GI on a litter. One MP took his place as the point man, the other brought up the rear.

Before leaving the temporary camp, one guard called me out.

"You tell the prisoners to take turns carrying the litter. Four in front of the litter and six carrying it; and take turns."

A sergeant guided us over the dark mountain trail. Carrying the wounded man felt strange. He must have been sedated and was covered with blankets. I sensed the warmth of his body through the blankets; once in a while he moaned. I hoped he would survive.

After two hours, we arrived at a field hospital. We prisoners were ordered to the side of the road and not long after, a 2-½ ton truck came to take us farther back. We drove for some time, encountering heavy traffic coming towards us. *Remarkable, they all have lights on. Obviously, they did not have to deal with our airplanes.* There must have been hundreds of trucks, or so it seemed. My heart sank. *The war is lost, too many supplies going to the front. No wonder we could not hold them.*

After a long night, we arrived at dusk in an open field, got off the truck and sat down to rest. As the sun came over the mountains, we discovered German prisoners scattered across the field. During the day, we were interrogated and our names and personal data taken. The interrogator gave each of us a card to fill out, which was eventually sent to our families by the Red Cross. Thus my parents finally learned that I was a prisoner of war.

While we were waiting around, we saw some trucks nearby, loaded with lumber. The personnel were all black. For the first time in my life I saw black people. They called us over to help them unload the trucks. While we were working, I realized how weak I was, not having had anything to eat for days; and still there was no food in sight. By then I was dizzy if I got up too fast.

When not working, we sat along the banks of small ditches irrigating the field. The sun was still warm, so we could take our shirts off. Killing lice became our only pastime; they really had become a plague.

The days went by, and still no food and water. Slowly the black engineers erected a fence around us, and the Italian "heroes" appeared as guards. On the second day, Hubert showed up.

"Where did you come from? Where did they catch you?" I asked.

"I hid behind enemy lines for three days but, eventually, I realized I could not make it back to our lines and gave myself up."

He was just as hungry as I and hoped that he could have something to eat at the camp. We were becoming weaker although we hardly moved. In the evening, finally, we were called to line up for food. Each one of us received a can of C-ration. These rations consisted of three different contents: two, we called "heavy", with cans of pork and beans or corned beef hash; the third, we called "light." The light ones contained a few crackers, some instant coffee and, maybe, some candy.

Every box with cans included small can openers. I was in a dilemma, in the haste of my surrender I forgot to take my mess kit; so no spoon. After I had opened the first can, I bent the lid a little in shape to make a primitive but useful spoon. A few days later, I found a piece of wood and a nail and fashioned a handle for the spoon.

From then on, we received a light can in the morning and a heavy ration in the afternoon. Another well-received improvement was a waterline that engineers extended into the camp.

German officers lived in a tent near the gate. They received much better treatment than we pawns. Our resentment grew when we saw one of the officers go into the tent with an armful of white bread. As we started to throw rocks at our former superiors, the MPs came to quiet us down. The next morning an announcement informed us that, because of our behavior, we would not get any rations for the day. Our esteem for officers had never been too high, but now it was at rock bottom.

Slowly, we settled into a routine. The prisoners had divided into two groups. Soldiers of the army drifted to one side and the Luftwaffe, including us paratroopers, to the other side.

After about a week, we were issued pup tents.

Hubert, an old hand at out-of-door living, reconnoitered a slight elevation in our row.

"Bert, get as many sheets of cardboard as possible from the dump."

"What are we going to do with cardboard, and why do you always send me?"

"Because if you don't get the cardboard, you will have a wet ass for the duration of the time we are here. Besides, you have younger legs than we old-timers."

Four of us were assigned to one two-man pup tent, which meant that we had to lie sideways next to each other. The unwritten law was never to touch the inside of the tent since it would draw moisture when it rained. The pup tent was so narrow, we could never stretch our legs. It rained almost daily now. I appreciated Hubert's foresight to look for a slight elevation and a good layer of cardboards under us.

The days turned into weeks. Daily routine rotated around one light and one heavy can of C- rations, and the rain. The ground was soaked. When some of the drenched tents collapsed, the inhabitants spent their time at the open latrine during the rain. A solid wooden roof topped this structure and shielded them from the rain until they were dispersed among other tents. Now I shared the pup tent with five men.

At least, we did not freeze during the nights thanks to the issue of one blanket to each prisoner. By now we knew the most intimate details of each other's lives. Our main topics were: number one, sex; number two, food.

One of the men in our tent was a former mess sergeant, May. He had an unpleasant personality, but he liked to talk about food. He bragged that he could put a gourmet meal together on his *Gulaschkanone,* a portable kitchen called goulash cannon. May did not like me and always called me *Rotzlöffel,* snotnose. I was the youngest and had the lowest rank in the tent, so I had to keep my mouth shut.

One evening was topic-one night, when the old–timers bragged about their conquests.

"And, what about your experiences with the ladies, Snotnose?" May asked.

"Oh, I've met a few girls."

"Bert, why don't you tell about your kissin' cousin, Annie. The one from Bornlieb," Hubert said.

"I told you that in confidence," I complained.

"Come on, tell those old Casanovas anyway." He chuckled.

"Well, it was during my time as a Luftwaffenhelfer. On my weekend leave, my mother sent me to get some black-market food items from distant relatives in Bornlieb. So far, the authorities had not stopped any soldier in uniform to check for contraband.

"Annie was the daughter of the relatives and about two years older than I. Her family put me to work on the farm for the day. At night, I slept on the couch in the parlor. I was barely asleep when I woke up to see a figure in a nightgown standing next to me.

"Move over," Annie said.

"She took the blanket off me and said, 'Don't you have a nightgown? Oh well, mine is big enough for the two of us.'

"The next morning Annie was gone," I said.

"Okay, Snotnose. Give us some details."

"Well, the night gown was big enough for the two of us."

"I don't believe you. You have a vivid imagination. Whoever slept two in a night gown? You would not get in."

"It had two big openings, one at the top and one on the bottom."

"I still say you are lying."

"You can say what you want, I remember the night well."

With that I turned and hoped to fall into a deep, uninterrupted sleep without dreams about our present situation.

Sergeant Miskewitz was one of my tent companions. At first he did not make any impression on me, but during our conversations I learned that he called himself "the undertaker of Nettuno." Miskewitz was in charge of a group of the Penal Battalion, soldiers who were used for dangerous tasks, such as digging up mines or duds. Those assignments were their sentences after they had been court-martialed for severe crimes. At Nettuno, they collected the bodies of Allied or German troops killed during attacks and counterattacks in the previous months. Asked about the smell and how he could stand it, he replied, "I was drunk all the time. They supplied me with all the liquor I wanted." His stumbling around in no man's land must have been some sight. Miskewitz had turned into an alcoholic and missed his bottles badly.

Lying in the tent for days, Hubert and I talked about our hometowns and relatives. Even religion came up.

"Is your village also divided into Protestants and Catholics?" Hubert asked me one day.

"Actually, we had only one Protestant family living in our village, the rest were Catholic. This goes back to the Thirty Years' War in the 17th century."

"Yes, that was the War of the Reformation," Hubert interrupted, "when all the inhabitants of a village had to be of the same religion as the owner of the land."

"My oldest known ancestor was born in 1621. He must have gone through hell in his life," I added.

"Yeah, probably much the same mess we are in now," Hubert remarked. "Did you belong to the diocese of Limburg as we did?"

"No, we belonged to the diocese of Trier; the town is going back to Roman times. I had an uncle who was a bishop in Trier. He died some years ago and is buried in the Trierer Dom, the cathedral. We went there several times and I learned a lot about it."

Now Hubert became excited, "I remember now, there is some big building and they call it the Porta Nigra or the Black Gate."

"When we were there we saw all those old buildings," I said. "Actually, did you know that Trier is the oldest city in Germany? The Celts lived there already in 1500 before Christ, my father told me."

"Your father really knew about that stuff," Hubert exclaimed.

"Yes, he liked history and teaching me about it. Even his trade was based on a historic system, the Guilds. For years he learned to be a cabinetmaker with his great-uncle, who was my great-grandfather. After his apprenticeship, my father traveled all over Germany as a journeyman. Before World War I, he worked in Kiel, Northern Germany, when Germany built up her fleet."

"Didn't you once say that you had relatives in Bad Assmannshausen?" Hubert wondered.

A call to pick up our C-ration, a heavy can, interrupted our reflection.

"I'll tell you more about my family later. Food comes first in this hellhole."

"I wish there'd be enough of it for a change. One can in the afternoon, weighing only six ounces, is barely enough to keep you alive, and the light can in the morning is just good enough to make you hungrier. I get woozy just getting up too fast."

Trechtingshausen: My hometown in the 1930s.
All the boats were moored along the bank when not used to cross
the Rhine to work in the vineyards visible top of the picture.

My paternal grandparents, left.
My maternal grandparents, right.

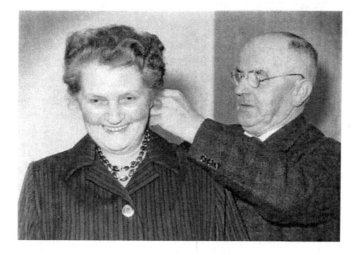

My parents.

MY ANCESTORS AND ME

"Yeah, those C-rations will never make up for the days without food before I got here," Hubert said, as we sat near our pup tent. "Go on, I asked you about Assmannshausen."

I had taken my shirt off and was busy looking for lice along the seams. These pests were really getting to me. Every dry day we sat near our tent and hunted for them. Twenty-five to thirty was a good day's result. My thumb nails were always bloody from squashing these buggers between them. I didn't give a damn how it looked. By now we were dirty beyond description. I figured it must have been four to five weeks since I last washed my hands and a shower was months in the past.

"My mother's family is from there. The Kilians in Assmannshausen were an old teamster family, who had teams of horses to aid the ships through the rapids. The three Kilian brothers, Christian, Karl, and Philip, lived there. Onkel Philip was still a teamster but transported mainly wood they made vinegar from, and he also had a team of horses pulling a carriage to take tourists up to the Niederwald monument. Later he switched to a motorcar."

"I can't believe you remember your family tree so well," Hubert said. "We lost track of the generations before my grandparents."

I explained that in our area many inhabitants inherited vineyards. If those couldn't support families with their harvests, men learned a trade and traveled as journeymen, but they usually returned to their village to become vintners.

"When I was young," Hubert remarked, "I took a trip on the Rhine on a side wheeler, I remember miles and miles of vineyards

15

along the mountains on both sides of the river. Do the Metzroths have vineyards?"

"Yes, on the left bank in Trechtingshausen and on the right in Assmannshausen. The towns lie diagonally from each other. For years, their people traded–and often found their spouses–across the river."

"That's a good way to increase your holdings, huh?" Hubert joked. Looking up at the approaching clouds, he continued, "Time to line up in our sardine can again. We'll get less wet there."

I stopped the lice hunting, put my shirt on and crawled into our tent. This procedure had to follow a certain ritual. The inside guys crawled in first, followed by the outsiders. Each of us had received a blanket; and in cold nights we spread two blankets over all of us. We outsiders doubled our blanket to keep warm. With the meager rations one didn't have to go to the latrines at night, that avoided troublesome commotions.

While reminiscing with Hubert about the area I called home, I chose to forget our plight and thought about my family. Now I knew no better way to deal with the discomfort, and the smell of six unwashed bodies in their dirty, damp uniforms, crammed together in a two-man tent.

Was my family already in the ever-increasing war zone? What were they going through now? When would they learn I was no longer at the front? Having no answers to my questions, my thoughts retreated once more to the past.

Individuals are struck by tragedy even in the absence of war. My mother's father was Christian Kilian from Assmannshausen; he married Katharina Kloos from Trechtingshausen. When my mother was one year old, her father drowned in the Rhine. Although he had helped his brother-in-law, Lorenz Kloos, to run the stone quarries, the latter refused to compensate my grandmother or give her any assistance.

She lived alone with two little girls, trying to make a living by cleaning houses and taking in laundry. Mother told us about those times of destitution. She was quite resentful toward her uncle who reaped his true reward when another relative cheated him out of his business and left him in poverty.

My real grandfather had a brother, Karl, who had lost his wife. Eventually my grandmother married him. Karl was a blacksmith. He was a skilled artisan in the trade. To this day the iron fence he crafted for the churchyard in Assmannshausen still stands.

In addition to his trade, Karl worked also as a vintner and had many vineyards. One of these was in the well-known wine-producing area of Assmannshausen, the *Höllenberg.*

I don't remember much about Karl Kilian. He died when I was four or five years old. Before I was born he gave up blacksmithing and built a house *im Stich*, a site on the way to Aulhausen, where cousin Thilo later had a restaurant.

The Kilians lived off their wine harvest and also ran a bed-and-breakfast. When Opa Karl died, Oma continued the B&B for a while. My sister Ina spent a lot of time in Assmannshausen to be company for Oma Katharina.

My reminiscing was interrupted by Miskewitz, talking again about topic number one, girls, consistently recalling his trips to the whorehouses.

He started to talk to me, "You don't know anything about that, huh?"

I was getting a little pissed off about his always belittling me. "I never had to *pay* for these activities."

"As if you had any experience," he retorted.

I had to shut him up about the needling. "When I was in the antiaircraft unit last year, just turning seventeen, we had ample opportunity for this. In Germany, most of the men were not at home. I had good thirtyish-year-old teachers."

That did the trick.

I was born on 20 September 1926, the third child of Nikolaus and Christina Metzroth. My older siblings were Ina and Karl. At that time, we lived upstairs in the house of my paternal grandparents in Trechtingshausen. The older Metzroths occupied the first floor. I spent parts of every day with them, especially with my grandfather. After he suffered a stroke and was partially paralyzed I could not understand that he could not move his arms and legs properly. Before, we always had such a good time together. When he died a little later, I saw my father cry for the first time.

Next to my grandparents' house was their huge barn where they stored firewood and hay. The hay for the two goats, though, my grandparents kept in the lower part of the house. Adjoining the stable was the outhouse.

During the day, I had no problems going there but when it was dark I always required the aid of my older brother, Karl, because I could not reach the light switches. Once he had me stranded at the outhouse. The total darkness and the eyes of the two goats glowing in the dark were too much for me. My piercing scream alarmed my grandmother upstairs and she immediately rescued me.

Karl was not mean, but I can understand the temptation to do this trick at least once. Grandmother took me upstairs and consoled me with her specialty, peppermint tea with a lot of honey in it. When my aunt Louis was present, who did not like us kids, Oma put an extra load of honey into the tea to spite Aunt Louis. I never knew then why my aunt was so odd around us. Later I learned that she and my mother did not care too much for each other.

In the old days, Trechtingshausen was the last stop for ships on the left bank of the Rhine before the *Binger Loch* with its very dangerous rapids. For this reason, Trechtingshausen became a busy place. Crews emptied, or partially emptied, the ships to facilitate the passage through the rapids. Horse-drawn wagons delivered the removed cargo to Bingen, the next larger town, where the barges picked up the cargo again after safely passing through the rapids. All captains preferred to navigate the Binger Loch with a reduced load; some used the reverse approach: They came back to Trechtingshausen with the empty wagons to collect the remainder of the load.

Think for Yourself

One of the oldest buildings in Trechtingshausen was called the *Salzhaus*, a warehouse for the salt shipments coming up the river from the sea before being further distributed into the hinterland. Another interesting building, dating back to the 16th century, was the Tithes House in Assmannshausen, acting as the Internal Revenue of our time. There, the tithes were stored, or one tenth of people's income. My maternal grandfather, the blacksmith, owned the house. My mother spent most of her youth in this historical landmark, which is still standing today.

My parents and my maternal grandmother built a house in the *Lohkaut.* In earlier times, this was a place where tanning bark was collected for further use. Loh was the bark of small oak trees that were chopped down and their bark peeled off. Even in my youth, this bark was still used to preserve materials such as sails and lines, to prevent their premature decaying. Kaut means a hole in the ground or a container in the ground to accept the Loh for processing. I watched how men applied these old and true methods to alleviate prevailing poverty in our region. After WWII, when new jobs opened in other areas and commuting by train became easier, this tanning system became obsolete.

When widowed, Oma sold her house in Assmannshausen, and moved in with us. With my mother's help she continued a profitable B&B business. We children had to give up our rooms for guests during the summer. Oma, Karl and I lived in the attic for the duration of the season. I spent half the night under the sheets to escape the mosquitoes. When everything was quiet I heard the rushing of the river. Years later, I had renovated the attic into an apartment; then Veit, my son, was probably lulled to sleep by the same sound of the river heard through the open windows.

The Rhine played an important role in my youth. From our house, beyond the railroad tracks, was Trechtingshausen's beach, a stretch of sand at the bank of the river that lured local youths to swim and frolic. In the summer, I literally lived there. We took our Saturday bath in the river. One day, Aunt Louis scrubbed me, using handfuls of sand. Pulling my pants down, she discovered five or six streaks across my rear. Immediately she asked me, "What did you do in school?" Adults always know! I had not diligently exercised my reading. My stumbling block was the word *"Krummstab"*, a staff the bishops use. Well, the teacher, *Herr Külzer,* said, "Let me introduce you to another staff." The bamboo left the red streaks. The lashes hurt like the dickens, but it was a matter of honor not to cry, which usually earned you another two or three blows. The screamers got less.

In the first grade we practiced our lessons on wood-framed slate boards. One side of the slate was for writing, and the other for arithmetic. To correct any mistakes we had a sponge and a rag. The sponge was supposed to be wet. The girls always carried a wet sponge, the boys used spit, which had a tendency to grease up the slate eventually and refuse to accept writing with the slate pen. It started to smell, too. One day my mother wiped out my whole assignment,. She scrubbed both sides down, squeaky clean; I had to do my homework over and from then on I had a wet sponge. Well, most of the time. I can still remember sitting on the front sandstone steps of our house, and sharpening the slate pen by rubbing it on the steps.

A year later we graduated to pen and ink with inkpots recessed into our desks. The teacher foiled the temptation to dip the girl's braids into the ink by placing the girls in the rows behind the boys.

I mentioned before my total attraction to the Rhine. The river captivated me with the ships passing by, and above all, the *Nachen,* the boats used to cross the Rhine to work in the vineyards.

The older Nachen were wooden vessels. In the 1930s, however, the local blacksmith started to build them from sheet metal. In his first models he used rivets, but later he welded the sheets together.

From the day my father bought one of the sheet-metal Nachen, Karl and I *lived* in it. Our boat had a sail, which we only hoisted when the wind was blowing upstream to prevent the swift current from carrying us downstream.

Our spritsail was primitive compared with regular sails. We lowered the sprit and wrapped the whole sail around the mast, which was set through a hole in the mast bench. When we went home, we could easily lift mast and sail out of the bench and take it with us.

Since the board with our Nachen registration number was removable, Karl and I took it off whenever we engaged in daring exploits involving the steamer tugs coming upstream. We tried to get as close as possible to the side-wheelers. To make it interesting, we stuck a beanpole into the thrashing wheel. Sometimes the crew chased us with a bucket of dirty water, but the men could not identify us.

Trechtingshausen vintners who did not own boats boarded the ferry, which transported them to their vineyards. Most of the time, however, the ferry's engine did not work. If that was the case, the usual solution was, "Get the Metzroth boys to take you over."

We knew every regular ship on the Rhine. The logos of the shipping companies were banded around the smoke stacks and identified the owners. We already called out the names of the white fleet of excursion steamers' names when they came around the bend. In the 1930s, few vessels had diesel power. In contrast to the side-wheelers' noisy thrashing of the water, the steam vessels with propellers produced only a slight hiss when operating.

I was frequently hanging out at *"Tante Lene's,"* aunt Lene's. She had four boys, all older than I, neat guys. They were always building something. Joseph, Tante Lene's oldest son, shot to death by the Soviets after the war, always took me under his wings. He had built a paddleboat and often invited me for rides in it.

One Sunday after church, Joseph asked, "Shall we go out in my boat?"

"Sure," I said.

I was ten at the time and had my first communion that year. When I climbed into Joseph's tippy boat in my blue Navy suit, we capsized.

I can still hear him laughing. He said, "Go home to my mother, she will dry you out."

Tante Lene laughed, too, when she saw me. She stripped me, gave me old swim trunks to wear, rinsed my suit in clean water since the Rhine water was dirty, and dried the suit; afterwards she ironed it. Tante Lene always helped.

I went home and nobody would have known the difference, but the village gossip had already informed my mother. She appreciated the quality of the ironing, did not scold me but only told me to change clothes before the next time I wanted to go paddling.

Tante Lene was quite influential in my life during the war. More about that later.

When I was thirteen years old I rebuilt a rowboat, mostly at the expense of my grades in school. Three of us boys found it upstream in the shallows of the Rhine River. One of my friends, or so I thought, was fifteen-year-old Walter Weber, a good soccer player who later went down with the *Bismarck*. The other one, also fifteen years old, was Werner Fendel. He perished on the Russian front during the brutal winter of 1943.

We dragged the boat ashore. Its stern was missing, chopped off by a side-wheeler. This wreck we loaded on a cart and took it to our house.

"What is that in front of my workshop, good to break up for firewood?" my father asked when he came home from work.

"I will put a new transom on it," I promised.

"Not with my wood," my dad said.

Walter and Werner promised to help me with the rebuilding of the craft but never showed up. So I had to prove to the world that I could do the job myself. But where to get the wood for the transom?

An old work shack next to the railroad dam, long abandoned, was to be my wood mine. The boards were impregnated with creosote and rather heavy. I could not move them over the road, so I had to find another solution.

Aha! In a passage under the railroad track is a gully, as nice a gully as could be: swampy bottom, only three feet high, full of spider webs and with a gully odor.

On the other end of the pipe, next to the highway, I had parked my innocent cart. With a rope I dragged the pilfered boards through the gully and up the hole before I loaded them on the cart. Innocently pulling the load of boards on my way home, I noticed the appreciating glances of the burghers, "A nice boy, helping his dad."

The boards were muddy; a hose helped getting rid of the mud…but not the smell. Mother was used to these episodes of boy's adventures and their connected *aromas*. I had my boards and could finish the restoration of our boat. The consequence was an F in Latin; a minor loss in my estimation at the time.

My favorite book at that time was *The Black Corsair* by Emilio Salgari. I read the story several times. The corsair named his ship *Folgore,* lightning. *A fitting name for my boat.* But my *Folgore* never lived up to its speedy name.

When I launched the boat, it leaked relatively little. Of course, my two "friends" showed up at the launching and wanted to partake in the fun. "You should've helped. You lost any chance for a partial claim."

I was getting bored, just rowing or sailing the wooden skiff. There must be different means to propel the boat. Boats have screws to propel them. But to move the propellers you need engines; out of reach for me. The skiff is too small for a motor anyway.

The thought was taking hold of my life: How could I rotate the prop fast enough to have an effect on the movement of the skiff? Tugboats have slow-rotating screws, but they have steam to run them; they also have BIG propellers.

How to combine a slow-rotating power plant with a big screw, if the only power plant in the boat was me? How does one put screws into wood? A hole is drilled first with a drill bit, and to run the drill bit one needs a drill brace.

In my youth, braces were still in use since the electric drill was not yet common. My father had an old brace in his wood-working shop. So, how to install the brace and the propeller shaft in the boat? I did not have a stuffing box and did not want to drill a hole in the hull anyway.

Army engineers have attack boats where the engine is mounted on the transom!

Gradually, the plan took shape. I could rotate a brace; connect it to a three-foot metal rod, which rested in a two-prong device inserted into the rudder gudgeon. A washer, held by a nail through the shaft, prevented the shaft being pushed forward; another nail stopped it from being pulled backward by the force of the propeller.

Where could I find a big propeller? A large, rusty, round bottom of a can, almost a foot in diameter, was the answer. The wide propeller should compensate for the slow rotation of the brace. I formed a three-bladed prop, drilled a hole in the middle and fastened the screw onto the shaft. A hefty angle of the blades would have the tug-boat effect of a slow-rotating shaft, I figured.

I planned the trial for the next day. After a sleepless night, I was ready for the launch in the morning. The old timers, always present when something new was on the horizon, were laughing about my contraption. *I hope it works. They would have laughed about Michelangelo's ideas.*

After I had installed my invention, I readied the oars in case of dysfunction and shoved off, lowered the prop into the water and slowly rotated the brace. *The boat moves!* The spectators gradually disappeared leaving me alone with my creation. They did not see that, when I rotated the brace faster, the thin metal of the prop folded because of the heavier pressure on the blades.

Back to the drawing board. *I need a heavier metal for the blades.* The local blacksmith sold me a sheet of scrap metal for fifty *Pfennig,* and I was in business again.

I had a great time using my propeller-operated skiff when it reached speeds as if propelled by oars. Nevertheless, I always had the oars ready.

Over the years, I forgot Latin, but will never forget my brace-operated-tugboat-propeller-equipped skiff.

Because of the minor leaks I had to beach my boat every night. One morning it was gone. As I looked around, I saw the stern just penetrating the surface about ten yards out in the Rhine. With my dad's boat I salvaged mine.

Once I had pulled it onto the beach, I discovered four big holes drilled into the bottom of the boat, and a big rock in the bow to help it sink. I guessed that the boat must have turned over, the anchor fell out and held the boat in place. Although I suspected who the culprits were who wanted to sink my boat, I could not prove it. I repaired my *Folgore* and, for a time, I had a lot of fun with it.

After a few weeks, I found a huge rock lodged in the bottom of it. This time the damage was irreparable. Dad and I chopped my *Folgore* up for firewood; a sad end for the first in a row of boats I owned in my lifetime.

I spend a carefree boyhood due to my parent's open-mindedness and was not much aware of the developing undercurrents. The first political event I remember happened while we were still living in my grandparents' house in 1933: The Nazis came to power. On the morning of the elections I was awakened by a commotion downstairs.

"What is going on?" I asked my grandfather.

"Look across the river," he said.

I eyed the big retaining wall for the railroad and read this message in enormous lettering, *"Mit Hitler für Frieden und Gleichberechtigung,"* with Hitler for peace and equal rights. This slogan was visible for years after the war. Authorities tried to remove it, but the whitewash must have penetrated the rock. We knew where to look and saw as a ghostly reminder for the initiated a sign of the horrible past.

During the regime of the Third Reich, January 30th was celebrated as *"Tag der Machtübernahme,"* the day the Nazis took power. Only after the war did I realize the dilemma my father must have been in because of his affiliation with the Zentrum Party, the forerunner of today's CDU, or Christian Democratic Union. My grandfather was the *Bürgermeister,* or mayor, of Trechtingshausen at the time but was soon replaced by a party hack. New titles were initiated, such as *Ortsgruppenleiter,* political leader of the precinct or village. While friends and acquaintances used to greet each other cordially with *Guten Morgen, Guten Tag, Guten Abend,* Good Morning, Good Day, Good Evening, they now had instructions to say "Heil Hitler."

Most of the people retained the old greetings to the consternation of the Brownshirts. As kids we realized the tension in the village, and of course, to annoy these men and women, we greeted them with the old *Guten Tag.* It was strange, but the majority of men and women who now suddenly gravitated to the top had not been too successful before.

The Nazis could not make great inroads in the small communities; we considered the Nazis to be atheists. Because Trechtingshausen had no Jewish residents, the village was not involved in the persecution of Jews. We must judge the village people by the standard of *those* days. The inhabitants had not participated in any concentration camps; they were so distant from those camps that people were ignorant of what was happening since reports pertaining to this outrage did not appear in local newspapers.

The only event I remember that could be related to atrocities was a bishop's letter that was read from the pulpit. My parents talked about it, condemning the euthanasia occurring in a monastery serving the mentally retarded just across the Rhine in Aulhausen. This was so close that the news could not be swept under the rug.

All young people between the ages of ten to eighteen belonged to the Hitler Youth movement. From ten to fourteen, boys were part of the *Jungvolk,* or young people, as *Pimpfe,* similar to the Cub Scouts.

At fourteen we were inducted into the regular Hitler Youth. Unlike units in bigger cities, we had no political leadership in our small village. Some marching and singing, sports activities and, of course, introduction to war games were the only activities. Due to our knowledge about boats we became part of the naval youth movement. We did our exercises and drills in an old lifeboat. One of our leaders was sent to Kiel for two weeks of training on the school ship *Horst Wessel,* which is now the U.S. Coast Guard vessel "Eagle." I was promoted to *Oberrottenführer.* Sounds important, but I was only in charge of three boys younger than I. Uniforms were mandatory: in the summer brown shirts and black shorts, in the winter black jackets and long pants.

I had a close call with fate when one day an older leader came and told me he had to talk to my parents about opportunities for my future. I was quite honored and could not wait for him to see my parents. When we arrived at home, my father was at work and only my mother could talk to the representative. He explained that, due to my leadership qualities, I had a good chance to be admitted to one of the *Führerschulen,* or schools for future leaders. All tuition was free and I would have a good future as an officer in the SS. The Nazis started to recruit prospective leaders early. I was only fifteen years old and will never forget the moment, when suddenly my mother appeared ten feet tall as she told the leader, "No, he will never give up his faith."

He said he wanted to talk to my father; Mother said, "You will get the same answer from him."

When the leader left, I was mad at my parents for the missed opportunity to become an officer. Little did I know that my mother most likely saved my life and soul with her answer.

Lifeboat training in the Navy Youth movement.
Interesting history!
Furthest back on right, Leo, missing in Russia.
On left, Hans Josef, imprisoned for a long time for helping
German prisoners to escape from France.
On left second row. covered, Werner, died in Yugoslavia.
On right second row, Erich, prisoner of war in France, worked on
farm and married farmer's daughter.
On left front row, Eugene, died in 2007.
On right front row. Rupert A. Metzroth.

GROWING UP THE HARD WAY

In December 1942 the rumors in school started, "We are going to be inducted into the antiaircraft units."

At the time, I attended the high school of Bingen in one of two parallel classes that comprised the birth years 1926 and 1927. All the upper classes had already been inducted into the regular army and had suffered casualties on the Russian front. Our eagerness to become part of the military did not have much to do with patriotism but with the fact it was exciting and new. We did not think of casualties. Our parents' fears did not occur to us.

The rumors became reality in January 1943. Our two classes of about thirty students each were combined into one battery. Together we traveled from Bingen to Mainz for our induction as *Luftwaffenhelfer,* Air Force Auxiliary. At the railroad station in Mainz two sergeants greeted us. Forming easily into columns of three abreast, as we had learned in the Hitler Youth, we marched to the *Kaserne,* the German name for barracks. At this complex of numerous three-storied solid structures a first lieutenant met us.

"This is serious, no kid stuff anymore. You will now become part of the German forces."

Immediately the shouting and whistle blowing began. "To the *Kleiderkammer",* supply room, a German sergeant shouted. There we received our gear. We were shocked when the supply personnel handed us Luftwaffen-blue Hitler Youth uniforms, with Swastika armbands no less, instead of issuing regular uniforms. No more kid stuff? Rather than dealing with us as grownups the military treated us as *Pimpfe.*

No time to complain. Reality sank in. The only neat gear was the steel helmets. They were *prima,* great. No guns, no side arms.

Next we marched into a barn filled with straw and piles of blue-and-white-checkered cotton sacks.

"Take two of the sacks; fill one with straw for your mattress and the smaller for a pillow. Don't overstuff the mattress, or you will roll off it," the sergeant bellowed. "Afterwards you will report to your rooms for bunk assignments. Then you are free for the evening."

At 22:00 hours was *Zapfenstreich,* or taps. We fell asleep with the military smell about us: straw, leather, gun grease, and cheap soap, but, as yet, no dirty socks.

At six o'clock in the morning whistles and screams, *"Essenfasser raustreten!"* The men who had been assigned to pick up our breakfast grabbed the pitchers and took off for the mess hall.

They brought back "coffee", a watery brown drink, and *Kommissbrot*, the type of bread served in the German military, and jelly.

After our quick "hearty" meal we were called to fall in. The drills to break us down and have us submit to unquestioned obedience began. To our surprise and dismay, we were to salute not in the military style but had to use the Hitler salute with outstretched arm. This regulation seemed to pretend that sixteen-year-old youths were not soldiers.

Next, a *Hitler-Jugend,* Hitler Youth, leader materialized to indoctrinate us. We did not like it a bit. He must have realized that because he did not come back until we had assignments to our Flak, *Fliegerabwehrkanonen,* battery. There our CO, a brave lieutenant, told the political youth leader that his lectures interfered with our exercises. At that time the Allied air attacks increased steadily; our battery could not be missed in the defense of the Mainz-Frankfurt area for political lessons.

The battery was located in Budenheim, a suburb of Mainz. During the time of our training, we could go on leave almost every weekend because we were not actively deployed. Our high school teachers came to our battery to carry on with our academic lessons, which they held in the mess hall. A sergeant was in charge of discipline. Our teachers liked that, because we had never been more attentive. Interrupting the class resulted in pushups for punishment. The sergeant tapped the offender on the shoulder and gave the thumbs-down signal. Thumbs up or down regulated the pushups. During all this time the relationships among classmates was never better.

Our battery consisted of four 88mm guns, known by the Allies as *Ack Ack.* My position was K6, or *Kanonier 6,* gunner 6. The three aiming positions were elevation, horizontal, and my station, distance or fuse setting. Radar guided our night acquisition of the approaching aircraft. In the daytime, a four-meter distance-measuring scope calculated the target's position. We learned fast because we were eager and excited.

Sergeants were in charge of all equipment. The loading gunner was a Russian POW. We were not strong enough to push the heavy ammo into the breach at high elevation.

At the end of our training we shipped out to Franeker, Holland, to an antiaircraft artillery range. My buddy and I met Dutch girls our age and spent some time in nature. When we came back, our sergeant really chewed us out, "Don't you know you are in enemy territory and the area is full of guerillas who would have enjoyed slitting your throats?" That ended the romance; we left two weeks later anyway.

The war enveloped us after coming back to Mainz. In the spring of 1943 the air attacks happened in waves almost every night. The required military readiness put more strains on our schooling than before. Besides, the teachers' vacations started soon after our return to Mainz. No vacation for us.

At the end of summer, some of us, including me, were not promoted but sent home for a short reprieve. In the next wave of inductions, the years 1928 and 1929 were called up. We "repeaters" had to go through basic training twice because we were held back one year in school? My rebuilding a boat, and thus failing Latin, had done me in.

I was issued my equipment, uniform and gear, for the second time. In the military, you learn to keep your mouth shut and your second uniform at home.

This time, my assignment was to a light Flak antiaircraft 20mm battery. We were stationed only four miles from my home, protecting the strategic railroad switching station of Bingerbrück. My father was working there. It must have been awful for him to go into the shelter, knowing that his son was at the guns, protecting the station during a raid. Most of the time we were not involved because the planes flew too high for our small-caliber guns to reach them, so we played a lot of Blackjack. All of us had turned into seasoned sixteen-year-old vets.

Airforce Auxiliary,
Luftwaffenhelfer 1943.

STURM UND DRANG

Storm and Stress, the name for the literary period during the 18th and 19th centuries indicates the conscious awakening in Germany.

Goethe, the Renaissance man of the arts and sciences; Schiller, the leading poet of the time, and the philosophers Fichte, Hegel and Kant were well known throughout Europe. They stimulated the gradual beginning of critical thought. Many young intellectuals ran afoul of the establishment with their radical ideas, causing the revolution of 1848 in Germany. Military might crushed the people's uprising. Some of their leaders escaped to America, such as Karl Schurz, German-American statesman and soldier.

I hope it is not too presumptuous to compare this epoch with the time in which I was growing up. We did feel storm and stress, the awakening of our conscience, our dislike of the party officials who were certainly not individuals to look up to. In my case it was also the subdued but firm opinions of my parents that influenced my thinking.

I have mentioned *Tante Lene,* aunt Lene. She was an outspoken opponent of the Nazis. She had lost one of her sons in the battle of Crete. For this reason the officials did not dare to confront her. I suspect that she was also of the underground movement and might have supported fleeing persons. *Strangely, she always welcomed me in my uniform when these people were present.* It might have given her meeting an air of legitimacy with a uniform present. I suspect she listened to BBC newscasts because she was always well informed about the casualties on the Russian front. Our press seldom mentioned German losses.

We were reluctant to voice our opinions to others. Doubts always gnawed at our conscience. So many soldiers lost their lives; at least two or three obituaries a day announced their deaths in the regional papers. The Nazis could not sweep these notices under the rug. My cousin, Josef, was one of the first sailors of our village to die. He went down with his PT-boat in the English Channel. His brother, Willie, followed him in death two years later at the Russian front. Then came the announcements at school of the deaths of older classmates. By this time we tried to subdue all thoughts of defeatism. The only loyalty we felt was the love for family and admiration for our soldiers.

In 1943, Germany suffered two catastrophes: the fall of Stalingrad and the defeat of Rommel's army in North Africa. The authorities played down these events but the doubts remained. And here we were, my comrades and I, drafted into the service as *Luftwaffenhelfer*. After basic training we began to contemplate our situation. But we still had to be careful with whom we could share our thoughts.

My best friend at the time was Berthold Otto. We called him Negus because of his dark complexion. Negus had a beautiful singing voice. One of our group in the barracks had a record player and a vast collection of records. Many of these records were pre-1933. We listened to them at night before taps. To hear Negus singing along was an emotional experience. After all, we were only sixteen at the time and always a little homesick.

On weekend leaves, though, I did not spend too much time at my parents' house; I met Ruth, or better, she met me. She was twenty-one years old, blonde and, seriously, the runner-up in a national beauty pageant. She was bombed out, that means her family's house went up in flames during an air raid in the Ruhr Valley. Following that loss, Ruth and family moved to our village, where most of us admired her from afar. But, as I said, she met me. Many an evening or night, I floated home with a big grin on my face. My standing with the other girls was immensely enhanced.

When my brother, a sergeant in the 2nd Airborne Division, came home on leave, he was amazed at my conquest: his little brother and this beauty.

In late fall of the year 1943, the conditions at the front became ever more obvious: the German forces were in continuous retreat. The Allies had landed in Italy and soon battled our army at Monte Casino, and later at Anzio.

My brother and I had a long heart-to-heart talk about the political situation. He knew that I would soon be drafted into the regular armed forces. I had turned seventeen by then. Karl told me that the government was pushing to press as many of our age group into the SS as possible. We also heard rumors to that effect through the grapevine. What to do?

"If you volunteer for the air-borne troops, the SS would not dare to touch you," Karl said. "You have to go anyway. In the Luftwaffe you might end up in France or Italy and, most likely not in Russia." The German air-borne troops were part of the Luftwaffe. I volunteered.

Karl was right. On a December day in 1943, my comrades in the light Flak battery and I were assembled in the mess hall. In came a well-decorated SS officer to give us a patriotic speech. He had the German Cross, the Iron Cross, Close Combat Medal, the Wounded Medal, equivalent to the Purple Heart, in Silver, and two Tank Destroyer Badges on his sleeve. This badge was only given if the bearer had destroyed the tanks in close combat. He was impressive. We were in awe. This guy had been through the wringer. He asked for volunteers and many stepped forward, including Negus. Then he approached the ones who did not volunteer. Questioning our patriotism, he gave us a hard time. When he approached me I told him that my brother was a sergeant in the air-borne forces and that I had already volunteered for his outfit. I am sure that decision saved my life. Negus died in Belgium in 1944 under a hail of Allied bombs.

Not long afterwards I received my *Stellungsbefehl,* or draft notice, for the Luftwaffe and had my basic training in France, my third basic training. There is not much to say about my repeated drills, other than that I went through the same "breaking down and building up," just like a frequently remodeled home.

Since our training was in enemy territory and guerrillas were active all around us, we received five rounds of ammo for our rifles. They were supposed to protect us. After basic and jump school, I was off to Italy and the endphases of Anzio. Due to enemy air superiority we could only travel at night. The train brought us to Bologna and from there by truck behind the front line at Anzio.

After Basic Training.
4th Airborn Division, 12th Regiment.
On the way to Anzio.

Actually, we were near Nettuno. Nettuno and Anzio are twin cities. The German Forces were dug in near Nettuno and Allies near Anzio. Therefore, the Germans call it "the Battle of Nettuno," and the Allies "the Battle of Anzio."

Our company arrived at night. All our movements were at night. About a hundred of us were distributed throughout the battalion that had severe casualties and was down to about a hundred and fifty men. Most of us were new draftees. The three companies of the battalion, two light and one heavy, consisted mostly of old-timers who had been in action since the beginning of the war, starting in Holland, then in the Balkans, and recently in Russia. Their greatest success was on Crete. Now they inspected us cautiously. At first, these battle-tested men were not too impressed with the new replacements. The oldest of us was eighteen.

I was assigned to the heavy company, which, to my disappointment, was a bit detached from the front line. *There should be more action, other than a distant rumble or flashes.*

I asked an old-timer, "Is that all there is?"

"Count your blessings. They will start early enough in the morning," he said.

"Where is the front?"

"When it gets lighter you'll see a rise and that's where the action is."

In the morning, the company commander, a lieutenant, inspected us. He was surprised that we had already one year of service under our belt, at least where we *Luftwaffenhelfer* were concerned.

"If we only had some 20mm, we could make it hot for the *Jabos,* the fighter bombers that are giving us a hard time", the lieutenant said.

With the mortars, we were maybe a hundred yards from the front. Protected by a sharp rise before us, it was impossible for the enemy to reach us with regular artillery fire. Our company command post was nearby. For the first few days we did not have too much to do. Since we had two complete mortar crews for the two mortars, I was mainly used as a runner for the company.

Eager to go to the front line, I asked one of the old-timers to go with me and have a look. He was hesitant, but eventually he relented. Beyond the rise was a small plateau with a lot of trees, dropping sharply off into a ravine. My companion told me to keep low as we crawled closer to the rim. The guys in the foxholes told us to stay put; they noticed some activity on the other side. An observation ditch led right to the edge, shielded from the front by a rock but burrowed under the rock into the open. The opening was sufficiently covered so the enemy could not see it. This post was continuously manned to survey enemy lines about seventy-five yards across a ravine. Our line was about two yards higher than the enemy's.

I noticed a strange smell wafting in the whole area, a smell I will never forget.

"What is that smell?" I asked.

"You better get used to it. We have several dead in the ravine, some of ours and some of the Tommies. The British call these ravines wadis, an expression the Tommies brought with them from North Africa."

"I thought there were Americans across from us."

"No, they are farther south in the flatlands."

We were dug in at a relatively stable site since it was almost impossible to advance without incurring heavy casualties. That explained the bodies in the ravine.

I wanted to look into the ravine and also across to see, maybe, a Tommy. I worked my way forward, but before I could reach the edge somebody grabbed my legs and pulled me backwards.

"What do you think you are doing? You will get a bullet through your head, and then we have to shoot back, and then they shoot back and we will end up with more casualties just because of your nosiness. You will see them sooner than you like," my companion was swearing at me. "Let's go back before you start another world war."

"Okay, you don't have to be ornery about it!"

"They have a sharpshooter over there. We have not located him yet, but the man in the observation ditch is working on it. When we do, we put a machine gun in the ditch and empty a whole drum into him." Days later they got him.

My guide had a familiar dialect, almost like mine. "Where are you from?" I asked.

"A small village in the Taunus Mountains. You would not know about it, unless you are from the area."

"I come from the Rhine."

"That's a long river, what part of it?"

"Near Bingen, a little bit down the river from there."

"Hey, I come not far from there on the other side of the river."

"I have relatives across the river in Assmannshausen, Aulhausen and further inland, Bornlieb."

"That's my area! What are your kinfolk's names?"

When I mentioned their surnames, he did not recognize them.

"By the way, what is your name? Mine is Hubert."

"I'm named Rupertus, but everyone calls me Bert."

With this exchange started a long friendship that lasted through the war and through our time as POWs. This was not the last time Hubert saved my life. I was lucky to have had such a good *"Kamerad,"* a buddy.

Our lieutenant was not like some of the arrogant German officers I encountered. I heard that he was promoted through the ranks. Some months earlier he was a sergeant in our regiment, the 12th Airborne. Before that, the lieutenant had been wounded several times and had escaped from the Russians as a POW. He did not wear any medals, although I was told that he had a chest full. Being the company runner, I was often at the command post where he talked to us low ranks man to man.

The lieutenant was interested in our service as *Luftwaffenhelfer* and tried to requisition a 20mm antiaircraft gun for us. Before his request was answered, however, the Allies had broken through at Monte Casino and we were in danger of being outflanked. We had to withdraw, our main strategy from then on. Without air cover and lacking supplies, we carried out one strategic withdrawal after another. The good part of these maneuvers was, we could pick our point of resistance, hold it a few days or weeks and then withdraw to another point of defense that suited us.

Our officers considered potential points of vantage days before our retreat. Supplies were stocked there, such as ammunitions. We withdrew usually at night; it took the Allies a while to realize that we were gone and they had to scout forward until they reached our line of resistance. Their contact usually ended up in an ambush.

I remember one of those ambushes well.

In the middle of August 1944 we retreated to a valley in the foothills of the Appennini Mountains. The German forces had circumvented Florence, which, because of the many treasures in this city, was not defended. Thus Florence was already in American hands.

From the higher elevations we could overlook the entire area. A river was coming out of the mountains and flowed by a little village, separating it from the flats. The road led out of the village across a bridge into the valley our regiment was defending. We had time to dig us in properly before the first Allied scouts showed up. They cautiously stayed in the village.

Our lieutenant surveyed the whole area in front of us and picked the spots for our mortars. The strategy underwent thorough rehearsals at regimental headquarters where officers assumed that the Allies wanted to push into the valley and to the road that would lead to the pass in the mountains, Passo Futa. As a runner, I accompanied the lieutenant on his survey. The mortars were in a side valley, well protected from any artillery as well as direct fire from tanks.

With a one-meter-distance measuring scope he established the distance from our mortars to the various targets. I carried the *Zielstöcke,* or aiming sticks, red-and-white-striped metal rods, about a foot and a half long. The lieutenant named the targets and I had to place the sticks in line from the targets to our mortars. For each position he quickly announced the distance between the two. I had done this chore many times before. The old-timers always told me to do it because, as they said, I had younger legs to gallivant in the forefront. The men were "really old", at least twenty-four or twenty-five.

At the mortars the lieutenant told us, which charges to use. We had little doughnut-shaped explosives, olive green disks in a white fabric with a slit through it. These disks could be placed around the tail end of the mortar grenade. With different added charges we shot various distances without changing the mortar setting too much. So for every target there was a different stick and the corresponding distance and disk charge. He could order to shoot target A, B, C and D and give the distance charge.

"If the Americans are smart they will come at night and dig in beyond the plains," he said to me.

We waited another day before the Amis, as we called the Americans, appeared in the village. Our artillery was ready for them. The enemy pulled back a little, dispersed into the fields and dug in.

Our units had orders not to shoot to avoid disclosing our positions.

As I lay next to the lieutenant, he explained to me what he expected the enemy troops to do. Thinking that they would not come during the day, he and I moved back to company headquarters and had a last good hot meal before the dance started.

The next morning we were at our observation point with a field telephone connection to the mortars.

The Allies came during the day.

"Do you see those idiot officers making their troops come during the day? They should be court-martialed," the lieutenant said. "They are coming full strength over the bridge." He was livid. "Don't they have any regard for their men? They are walking into the trap with open eyes."

Some tanks supported the ground troops, rumbling over the bridge.

"Our 88s will take care of them and they will never make it back over the bridge. I think they believe that they will not meet with much resistance from us. But they should have scouted it better," the lieutenant growled.

He was still muttering under his breath about a turkey shoot and idiot officers. "We'll let most of the troops come across the bridge, and then open up on them with all we have. They might try to get back across the bridge, but we'll use one mortar to prevent their retreat. Our artillery will take care of them. They will not be able to do anything but dig in at the plains."

Thinking like a chess player, the lieutenant planned his moves and directed his mortars toward the diverse targets by telephone. I was in awe of the unfolding drama in front of me. The 88s held the tanks and the front line froze. We endured until the American artillery and planes decimated us and we had to draw back again.

After this battle we retreated and had a week's rest for regrouping on the other side of the pass. The Passo Futa was my destiny and the beginning of my trip to the United States of America.

Just arrived on the liberty ship "William Yancey"
This picture was given to me by Thomas B. Bunch, sergeant in
charge of the guards on board.
I was one of the few who did not have a cap.

ON BOARD A LIBERTY SHIP

Back in the POW camp near Livorno we heard the rumors, "There is a bunch of us going to be shipped to America."

My wishful thinking became reality the day we had to line up to hear the names called of those who were to leave for the States. Mine was among the first names because I was one of the first prisoners arriving in this camp.

"Pick up your gear."

I scurried to fetch my blanket, my spoon, and an empty C-ration can for drinking. All my worldly possessions.

Let's get out of here! I am more than ready to leave this hell of a mudhole.

Soon trucks pulled up and we were on our way to the harbor of Livorno; the English called it Leghorn. The port was full of ships unloading cargo. We were herded into a barge, which headed out into the harbor. A good-sized freighter came into view. *Must be empty, from the looks of it; the prop shows a few inches out of the water.*

I was excited about the change in my life and did not have trepidations about my future. The war was over for me and I was looking forward to seeing America. We were sent into the lowest part of the hold and were underway shortly after boarding.

The next morning our keepers allowed us on deck. We discovered that we were in the Bay of Naples.

After a brief stay in fresh air, MPs separated us into the first and second holds of the ship. Three hundred of us occupied one compartment but on a higher deck than before. In one corner were stacks of C ration cases for our food. At the bottom of the ladder stood an empty oil drum with a wooden lid: our toilet facility.

The next day we headed out to sea in a southerly direction. Allowed on deck again for a while, we could enjoy part of the trip across the Mediterranean. We also had our first opportunity to wash. With fire hoses rigged as showers we could scrub ourselves. We received special soap for the saltwater and flea and lice powder at this preliminary hose down.

Among us was a young, slightly retarded man with a non-healing leg wound. Everybody on board felt sorry for him. The guards must have relayed the wounded man's predicament to the captain who brought him sulfur powder. The immediate effect of the application impressed us; after a few days the wound started to close.

Our vessel arrived in Oran, North Africa, the following morning. The harbor was full of ships; it seemed that a convoy was being assembled and was waiting for a few stragglers like us before leaving for the United States. We counted over seventy freighters.

To prepare for the long voyage, our ship's carpenter installed some toilet facilities outside the top deck's railing. This contraption nearly resembled a boatswain's chair. About four to five feet wide, it had two holes and a railing around it to prevent a man from falling overboard.

The convoy left Oran under the protection of two corvettes, DEs. I had mixed feelings. *What about our submarines? Would they attack us?*

As we went through the Straight of Gibraltar we had our last look at Europe. A long Atlantic Ocean swell greeted us and with it seasickness. Fortunately, we could spend most of the time on deck; so it did not affect me too much.

The crew as well as German soldiers approached me several times to translate negotiations about the sale of personal items, such as watches. Usually, at the conclusion of the deals, I demanded my cut of two cigarettes; sometimes I succeeded, other times I was laughed at. The ship's purser was interested in purchasing as many watches as possible. The first time I entered his cabin, I was confounded by his size. As he lay in his bunk I estimated the purser's weight to be about three hundred and fifty pounds. With the movement of the ship, his blubber moved like Jell-O. He only gave me one cigarette per transaction.

On my "business" trips the sergeant in charge of the MPs usually accompanied me. His name was Thomas Bunch. We became well acquainted and often talked about all kinds of things. My English improved. There were other Germans who could speak English, but they were older and more reluctant, or usually not as flexible as I was. They might have been warned by some of the German sergeants not to become too friendly.

Our freighter was considered empty and therefore on the outside of the convoy. I don't know how many ships in the convoy carried prisoners; an interesting routine, however, developed. All ships with prisoners on board had work parties chipping rust for a few cigarettes per day or some fresh fruit. By the time the vessels arrived at their destination, their superstructures were in good paint condition.

One day, Sergeant Bunch who hailed from North Carolina asked me if I wanted to serve in the crew mess. *What a question! What a job!* Of course I would do it.

But first I had to be cleaned up a little. A shower, no saltwater, but fresh water and soap!

Then Tom collected some old clothes and shoes because mine were falling apart. He brought me a T-shirt, a pair of blue jeans, and a pair of shoes one size too large. A radio operator, Lacey, came along and helped with suggestions.

My new job transferred me into a totally different world. Everybody in it was friendly except one crew member who refused to be served by me and cursed whenever I came near him. I received the same meals as the crew. In my job I had to go across a corridor from the crew mess to the galley, pick up the ordered food and serve the individuals. After the meal, I cleaned the crew mess and was free until the next meal. I could go to the afterdeck, prohibited to the other prisoners, and talk to the guards who were off duty. My English continued to improve steadily. Sometimes Tom and I sat on the depth charges aft and had political discussions. He was patient with my indoctrinated ideas. At night, I went back to the second hold to sleep.

A group of high-ranking German sergeants approached me and pointed out that we were still at war; I should not get too close to the enemy. There could be severe consequences. This warning was a rude awakening. Frankly, for me the war was over and I just could not bring myself to think of the men on the back of the ship as enemies. Nevertheless, not able to sleep that night, I was torn between allegiance to my country and the new friends I had made. I thought about my father, who had so often carefully tried to explain tolerance and who had emphasized to me to think for myself. His counsel was brave and dangerous, since I could easily have turned him in during the years of total brainwashing.

I am following Papa's advice. He so often had told me about individual thinking, maybe I should start now.

I can't forget Eichberg's eyes. He was a little Jewish boy, about the same age as I.

In 1936 I was ten and in my first year of high school, where the classes had Latin names: Sexta, Quinta, Quarta, Lower Tertia, Upper Tertia, Lower Secunda, Upper Secunda, and the graduation class, Prima.

An upper classman had accosted Eichberg in the lavatory and pushed him into a stall. Peer pressure was great. Wanting to show my approval, I laughed. I had betrayed Eichberg. He looked at me helplessly and slowly walked out. He never came to school again

My father's instructions and my misguided action in 1936 ran through my head after the German sergeants had talked to me.

Think for Yourself

Would they treat me the same if we won the war, as the boys had reacted toward Eichberg? I asked myself. Were my conversations with Negus, my buddy in the Luftwaffen Auxiliary, really what we thought about the war? We couldn't trust any other classmate. And what about the blacksmith in our village? He was an old communist. His sons had been incarcerated but later had been released; Germans needed them in the service. I liked the old blacksmith and often hung around in his smithy.

In my youth, I always wondered whom I could trust. Papa must have had a difficult time. Why didn't he join the Nazi Party like the other fathers?

I asked him once to buy a four-color picture of Hitler and hang it in the parlor, but he said that the postcard was good enough; and why did he keep it in the drawer of our radio stand and only bring it out on Sunday mornings when the party guys came to collect for the war? Why did he put it back when they were gone?

Why did he make me go to the Jewish dentist? Was it because we always went there, as he said, or did he want to prove something to me but could not say it aloud?

He always stressed, "Think for yourself!"

Boy, I really could use him now to set me straight.

Can I talk to Hubert about this? He would tell me, wouldn't he, to hell with the sergeants, do what you want, giving me the same advice as my father did.

Gee, I am only eighteen years old and am supposed to think for myself. We never were supposed to do that, just follow orders, I thought. I followed orders for two years and look what I got. I lie in this stinking hold, trying to be patriotic?

Around me, they are all asleep and dream of their next heavy C-ration. To hell with them all. I'll think for myself tomorrow!

Then I remembered the Nazi organ, *Der Stürmer.*

"What about the *Stürmer* pictures about Jews torturing little Christian children?" I had asked Papa. "You could see it in black and white."

"Who took the pictures?" he countered.

"They were not photographs but old woodcuts and drawings."

Then he drew me a picture of an elephant with a head on each end and asked what I thought of it?

"That's impossible!"

"Paper is patient; you can put a lot of nonsense on it. Think for yourself!"

Papa had a lot of guts and what he could do, I can.

My father, Nikolaus Metzroth, always reading.

With this thought I finally fell asleep, dreaming of a two-headed elephant.

The next morning I happily served breakfast for the enemy. The sergeants did not approach me again. I am sure that I was on their *list*.

We prisoners had settled into a routine. Every morning some of the prisoners tied a rope around the toilet-oil-drum in the hold, heaved it up and dumped the contents overboard. One day, the rope slipped. What a mess.

The toilet facilities outside the railing worked well, especially after the crew installed a box with a lid between the two holes. Reason? Due to the continuous wind blowing from the bow to the stern, the used toilet paper was ending up on the bridge.

The ships plowed onward at a speed of, maybe, eight knots, governed by the progress of the slowest vessel in our flotilla. The corvettes circled the ships like sheepdogs. But they definitely could not protect the entire convoy. We were all praying that we would be spared a *U-Boot* attack.

After work, I had to change back into my uniform because the Americans did not trust me in civilian clothes. That was understandable. Nor did I want to annoy the sergeants. A German sergeant was always held in high esteem. In military life we had to salute him, the same as an officer. Except for the warning about my friendliness toward the Americans I had nothing to complain about our sergeants. The political bunch must have been from the Army and not the Luftwaffe, or they were just envious men.

I developed a good feeling for the crew and the vessel. Her name was *William Yancey,* a Liberty ship.

Years later, my wife and I visited our son, Veit, in San Francisco. We were strolling along the waterfront when suddenly a silhouette of a ship came into view.

"A Liberty ship. That's a Liberty ship," I called to Almut. I was almost breathless to see one again. I did not realize how much I liked the sight of it.

The liberty ship "Patrick O'Brien" in the San Francisco Harbor. I went on board and had a long talk with the crew.

The American public in general is not aware of the importance the workhorses of the Atlantic and the Pacific played in keeping the supply routes open for the U.S. military during WWII. I still take every opportunity to go on board of the *Patrick O'Brien* whenever I am in San Francisco. Then the World War II crew talks to me about their experiences during the war. I learned that once in a while a former German POW comes aboard with the same attachment to the ship and similar memories to mine.

The register of all Liberty ships shows the *William Yancey* was broken up for salvage in Singapore. A sad end for such a brave vessel, which I will never forget.

Our journey continued without any *U-Boot* alarm. I dreaded the time when we would land in the U.S.A. On board, I had my regular duties to perform. I had enough to eat and the sleeping in the hold was not bad since I could use my life vest as a cushion. The future was in doubt, and I never lived more for the moment, totally helpless and exposed to the whims of my keepers. What really helped me in this confinement was my youth.

I do not want to have to go through my experiences at the front ever again. There our world had shrunk to the size of a small group of buddies, never counting more than thirty to fifty men in the company. We certainly had no understanding of the greater political picture. We defended ourselves as well as we could. We made do with what we could get and tried to stay as comfortable as possible. I think well of my friends and am honored to have served with them. During our crossing, I had ample time to wonder about the future and remember the past.

One nice warm July day two comrades and I had been looking for food in a deserted house in Italy. I saw an old umbrella and took it with me. I don't know why I kept it. What a soldierly picture I presented, dragging the umbrella behind me. In my hands I carried ammo baskets and on my back the base plate of the mortar and my rifle. I hooked the handle of the umbrella on my belt in the back. It looked like a tail. My buddies did not rib me. They just grinned and let me be.

A few days later a rainy period started; I was the only dry soldier in our company. Whoever has been through the unpleasant conditions in the field for days in rain and a soaked foxhole can understand my feeling of relative comfort. Hubert shared my umbrella with me after a while. It served also as camouflage. After I threw a few branches on it and some handfuls of dirt, I had a comfortable little world. It is amazing how a world can shrink to the size of an umbrella. I cannot understand why the brass has not supplied the troops with them. Just kidding.

Now back to the convoy. The inevitable happened: a November hurricane. It could not have been worse. The ship did not have any ballast and was tossed about on the waves. One night, the vessel listed to one side. All three hundred prisoners in our hold slid to that side and ended up like one big snarl inside the ship. The scary part was that the ship did not right herself for quite a while. We heard commotion on deck. If she had rolled over, we would all have drowned. Finally, with the full-speed rumbling of the engine, the crew was able to turn her bow into the waves and she slowly righted herself.

The next day the storm had blown itself out, leaving only heavy seas. Tom told me that most of the members of the crew were at the lifeboats. Due to the expert handling by the captain, the *William Yancey* continued her voyage.

The storm had scattered the convoy; there was no other ship in sight. Fortunately, we were close to America.

STALAG USA

The *William Yancey* arrived at Norfolk, Hampton Roads, two days after the hurricane. Upon landfall we were ordered into the hold. It took a long time before we felt that we had entered the port. With the vibrations of the engine, its stopping and revving, the bumps of the tugs maneuvering the vessel into place, and the final crunching of the ship's sides against the dock, we knew we had landed.

By the time it had turned dark, we heard noises of cranes running out and boarding planks moved on board. Shortly afterward we received orders to assemble on deck. The MPs were gone and a new group of soldiers guarded us. Tom had given me his APO address and told me to let him know when I would be at my final destination.

I was shocked to see that everything was as bright as daylight. Lamps everywhere. I had not seen any bright lights in Europe since the beginning of the war in 1939 when blackout was the rule in Germany and her neighboring countries.

A long line of POWs snaked down the gangplank. As soon as the last one of us was down on the dock we heard a shrill German command voice. I had not heard such a sound since basic training. A German sergeant came into view in an almost new uniform, best described by the German expression *mit Lametta behangen,* or covered with silver Christmas tinsel. The edges of his collar and shoulder boards sparkled in the lamplight. He was screaming for us to line up in rows of three and come to attention.

That was the wrong thing to do to the old-timers. Some steamy curses emanated from our ranks. First of all, the sergeant's spotless uniform told us the man could not have been in action too long before he was taken prisoner. He was not acceptable to us. Anyway, his act did not go over well.

53

If POWs are ordered to do something they execute a certain movement that is probably shared internationally: a slow shuffle in all directions. Only after more shouted orders did we smelly, lice-infested, tired, hungry and angry warriors form into three rows, but definitely not at attention. Red-faced, the German sergeant realized he had used the wrong approach. He asked us to be quiet for some announcements.

"First, you will be going to take showers and then be deloused. Following that, names will be taken."

"Again?" some POWs shouted.

The sergeant continued, "After that you board a train, which will bring you to your destination."

"Where are we going?" we asked.

"I was not told to which POW camp you would be shipped."

The showers were heaven; hot water and soap. The delousing was effective. At that time DDT was still in use. A cylinder covered our faces when the entire body was sprayed with powder. There was an immediate effect on the little inhabitants; they went wild; after a few minutes they all died. Our uniforms underwent a thorough cleaning as well.

A well-run operation.

Next we had to pass a man with our arms raised. I asked Hubert, "What's this all about?"

"They are checking for the blood group tattooed under the right arm." All members of the SS combatants had their blood type tattooed under the arm. *What fate would await them?*

After finishing our check-in procedures, we marched to a waiting train and boarded it. As German soldiers we had been used to cattle car transports. Actually, for a long trip cattle cars are not too bad. A layer of straw lets you sleep stretched out more comfortably than in a passenger compartment. The seats in the American cars were upholstered, though, not like the wooden benches in most German railroad compartments.

We noticed some switching of cars, being attached to a regular train, and then headed out of the port. MPs took position at the end of every car. The unavoidable question to the MPs was, "Where are we going?"

"None of your business."

"When do we get something to eat?"

"When we're ready to give it to you."

Their attitude was hostile. Unlike our former guards, who had been through the same fighting mess we had, these MPs had not seen the bloody scrapes soldiers at the front go through. Gradually we ignored the guards. We were used to going hungry for a while.

The train rolled through the night. Well-lighted places amazed us. It seemed there was no war going on. I tried to sleep, but I felt so drawn to the window, I wanted to see something of the landscape. It finally sank in: this is America. I could not wait for daylight to see more.

The sun came up on our left side. We still did not know where we had landed; but one thing was sure, we were heading south. Tom had told me he was from North Carolina. *We might end up in one of those places.* Looking out the window I saw some advertisement and of course, the names of the stations we went through; but nowhere could we find out, through which state we passed. The train stopped at one of the larger railroad stations and, from a car's tag in the parking lot, we deducted we were in Virginia.

Finally the guards came with food, and with something I never had in my life, COFFEE. Real coffee, not the fake stuff, *Ersatz,* which we drank in Germany as long as I could remember. Sure, sometimes on Sunday my father and mother drank a cup of the real brew. It smelled good, but they told me I was too young and would get a nosebleed from it.

Along with the coffee came peanut butter sandwiches. *What is that stuff? Never heard of peanut butter. It really doesn't taste bad, especially on white bread.* For years we had eaten the dark military bread, half flour and half sawdust.

I was indeed in a new world. Take lunch, for example: sandwiches with, what looked like, *Fleischmagen,* Bologna, and some white stuff on it, which, I was told, was mayonnaise. *If things keep going like this, I must be in the right place. To hell with the guards and their attitude.* Conditions started to look up.

Soon we were in North Carolina by the looks of the number plates on the cars outside the station. *Is Tom home already?* Then South Carolina. So the states ticked off. It was dark by now and we were still going south. I tried to remember my geography lessons about America but did not remember what came after South Carolina.

The refrigeration building. The first building we saw of Camp Blanding. The railroad tracks were on the other side next to the forty warehouses.

Our train was moving south throughout the night. We woke up when our cars were switched around in a station called Jacksonville, Florida. Never heard of the place. It was warm there, compared with the cold in Virginia.

Slowly we headed west. At noon we stopped at a brick building on one side, and on the other, endless rows of warehouses. We saw soldiers outside in German uniforms, at least some of them, and others in American shirts and pants but with *PW* stenciled on their pant legs and the backs of their shirts. The German uniforms were the tropical kind.

Were those guys from the Africa Korps? A German sergeant greeted us with a friendly, "Welcome to Camp Blanding." The American guards were laid back, one in front and one at the rear, as they marched us to our new home over a little bridge and up a hill. The place seemed to be in the middle of nowhere, but peaceful.

View of Main Street from the gate.
On the right are the mess halls and administrative buildings
And on the left the washrooms, one per company.

We came to a halt at a big gate. On our way in, we were body-searched. More German POWs greeted us. Beyond the gate we stopped on a long, straight street. The right side showed long buildings elevated on cement blocks. On the steps leading into the structures stood POWs, welcoming us.

"Where did they catch you?"

"In Italy."

"You must have been in Monte Casino or Anzio. You really gave'm hell there."

"It was tough, glad to be here now."

A German first sergeant announced that we were temporarily assigned to the first company, a transition company. Later we would be distributed among the three regular companies.

"We first sergeants are in charge of what goes on inside the barbed-wire perimeter. The two rows of barracks behind you will be your temporary homes. There is a cot for each of you and on the cot are some gifts from us to get you started on your life here."

It sounded better all the time. Dismissed, we were eager to find out what the barracks were like. Inside every building stood five field cots. On every cot the newcomers found toothpaste, toothbrush, a comb, a small towel and, we could not believe it, a pack of cigarettes. We later learned that when the prisoners found out that we were coming; they had collected some script money from fellow prisoners and bought the items at the PX.

The barracks were small, square buildings, maybe fourteen by fourteen in size. The five cots stood along the walls; in the middle of the room a conical stove rested elevated on a sandbox. *This is better than the barracks we had in basic training.*

Through the intercom system an announcement informed us that supper was served for us in the long building across the street, which turned out to be the mess hall. The food was unbelievable. German food: potatoes, meat and vegetables and for desert, ice cream. I thought I was in heaven. These cooks were pros and their cooking was typically German. Sometimes the American commanding officer ate here.

My hutment for over a year.

We had the run of the camp. After supper we explored our new surroundings. Soon the Commandos, the work details, came into the camp. They asked a lot of questions.

"Where are you from in Germany?"

"You look too young to be in the service."

"How long have you been in the Luftwaffe?"

It went on and on. Most of the prisoners had served in the Africa Korps. They were captured in the spring of 1943.

At ten in the evening, taps sounded through the intercom, ending my first day of about fifteen months in camp Blanding. I called it *Stalag USA, Stammlager* or main camp, was the name of camps which housed enemy prisoners in Germany.

The hutments of Company 2.
My hutment was the fourth from the right.

Waking up to reveille at six-thirty in the morning was a new experience for all of us newcomers. No shrill whistle blowing and screaming? Anyway, we got up to face the new unknown day and lined up on Main Street in rows of three with enough space between the rows for a man to pass through. The American sergeant counted and reported to the officer of the day, "All prisoners accounted for, Sir."

Then the German sergeants read the orders of the day, such as assignments to work details. One German NCO and an interpreter were attached to each unit.

After headcount, we were dismissed to breakfast, where we met our first corn flakes and milk. *What kind of stuff is this? Looks like straw, but with some milk and a little sugar, it's not bad.* All the American food items were new to us, since we had been used to bread, margarine and ersatz coffee in the morning.

Because we did not have any assignments yet, we returned to our barracks. Before long we found our names on a posted list, "Metzroth, Rupertus, second company; Müller, Hubert, third company."

While Hubert and I bemoaned our assignments to different companies, we were glad to stay at Camp Blanding. About half of the POWs who arrived with us had to leave for outlying smaller camps.

I was to bunk at the number-five barracks. After I moved in, I had the feeling that I was not welcome. Perhaps Ernst Dammann, my detail NCO, would find a solution.

"Ernst, I am not comfortable with the guys in my hutment. I request a transfer."

"I'll see what I can do."

Soon I was able to move to Ernst's hutment, number four next door.

My first assignment was as an interpreter in the shoe-repair and tailor shop with Ernst as the sergeant in charge. We had to work the night shift of the tailor section.

As an interpreter I had very little to do. When minor adjustments had to be made to work or machinery, Mr. Carrier, the man in charge of the shop, told me so and I in turn informed Ernst of the new instructions.

There was a huge pile of torn barracks bags in a bin, which our detail had to mend. This heap was ideal for a nap. There were no interruptions since everybody had his job to do and a quota to fill. Mr. Carrier and his secretary soon left after we arrived at five o'clock. Jim, an American veteran of the North Africa campaign, took charge of our detail. He had been seriously wounded at Kasserine and was discharged from the U.S. Army. He had a good rapport with the German Afrika Korps veterans. His attitude was, "Don't rock the boat if everything goes smoothly." Despite his poor health, Jim hung in there as well as he could.

The night shift in the shoe-repair shop was a separate unit from ours in the tailor shop; but Jim did not have any trouble with the "cobblers" either. When I was not napping on the barracks bags heap, I ambled through the shop, talked to Jim or went outside the shop for fresh air or a cigarette. A guard was posted outside the building at the only exit, a small door in the huge hanger door. Usually the guard sat on one side of the door. We opened the door slowly so as not to startle the guard, said hello, showed him our pack of cigarettes and settled down on the other side of the door.

U.S. Army members had to pay to have their shoes resoled. Consequently the guard, armed with a shotgun, often came with a brown paper bag under his arm, which contained his or his buddy's shoes to be soled. If he was nice to us, I took the bagged shoes and smuggled them past Jim into the shoe shop, where I had them repaired by the shoe detail.

Sometimes, when Jim was in a good mood, he gave me a nickel for a coke. The atmosphere was congenial.

Our work quota was ten barracks bags per man, plus ten for the interpreter and ten for the NCO. Our detail consisted of eight tailors, the sergeant and me. We had to repair one hundred bags per shift and could finish this task in five hours.

There were about fourteen sewing machines in the tailor shop and I had ample time to examine them. At times I repaired some bags just to be busy.

Upon my experimenting with the electric sewing machines, I noticed that the flywheel of each machine rotated at a fairly good clip. *How could I put a fan on the wheel?* I rummaged through the trash barrels and found some very stiff cardboard boxes, which had contained the soles for the shoes. Measuring the largest diameter from the center of the wheel to the table of the sewing machine, I cut a disk to size and from the disk a three-bladed propeller, which I forced on the shaft, then I tightened the knurled nut on the propeller. Eureka! An instant cooling fan. I had the time to do it, so I installed fans on the other machines, too. The faster a man worked, the cooler and more comfortable he felt.

What we did not know was that a detail of civilian women worked the day shift. Reporting for work the next evening, we found a thank-you note for the fans plus some nickels for bottles of Coke. I felt like Edison.

When I later visited Camp Blanding in the 1970s after attending my youngest son's graduation from the USMC boot camp at Parris Island, South Carolina, the refrigeration building was still standing and so was the tailor shop. The laundry plant had been dismantled; only the smoke stack remained. Our old camp had disappeared.

I had noticed a man named Adolf in the camp. He became one of my roommates in Dammann's hut. Adolf was an old man, at least forty-five years old. He always walked around with a neck brace and appeared to be in pain. We felt sorry for him. I have never met a more interesting person in my life. As soon as he entered our hut he took off his brace but kept it close to him so he could immediately put it on whenever another person entered.

Over a period of time I became well acquainted with Adolf and his life's story. Eventually we all knew each other's stories.

Adolf was born in Czechoslovakia. His father was Czech and his mother German. Before the war he traveled as a hobo and landed in Marseilles, France. After drinking one night away, he woke up in Algiers, North Africa, in the French Foreign Legion. When a French plane made an emergency landing in the desert near Algiers, Adolf had orders to guard the plane. Several days later he realized they had forgotten about him. He lived of meager rations and water on the plane.

Eventually it occurred to the French: Adolf is missing, and then, where is the plane? They found him. He was relieved from his post. For staying under very hard conditions the French awarded him a medal.

When Adolf came home, the Czech Army drafted him at just about the time his namesake marched into the Czech Republic. The Germans took him prisoner. Now, because of his German mother, the German army drafted him. The North Africa campaign ended his career; he became a prisoner of the Americans and thus my roommate.

63

"See my medal here? I'll keep it in case I become a French prisoner," Adolf said.

The knowledge of several languages helped him. He was fluent in Czech, German and French, and spoke also Arabic and English. Adolf never volunteered for anything, but used his neck brace wisely. He was one of the first POWs released after the war. This man taught me a lot about life in general and was well educated in the arts and theater.

I was amazed at how many interesting personalitities I met as a prisoner. One man, a college professor, was outspoken about politics. This did not go over well with the hard-core Germans. One day we heard a ruckus on Main Street. Several of the German POWs cornered the professor and wanted to stone him. He took refuge in a culvert. The noise alarmed the guards at the gate. They rushed to rescue the prisoner. Of course, the stone throwers had disappeared in the meantime. The Americans regarded the professor as the troublemaker who was disrupting the tranquility of the camp. He was taken out of the camp and for some time lived in a small tent outside the perimeter. Then, one day, he was gone.

After this incident I was cautious about my knowledge of the present situation in Germany. I realized that the members of the Africa Korps did not know too much about the conditions in Europe and still believed in the *Endsieg,* the final victory. Most of us, who should have known better, trusted the tale of the *Wunderwaffe,* or wonder weapon. What that was, was everyone's guess.

We were allowed to write one letter every two weeks on an 8 ½ x 11 piece of paper. This sheet was heavily coated with a white substance so that, just in case one tried to write in invisible ink, it would dissolve the coating. We found it a pain to write on the paper because the pen clogged up after every few words. At least, I could write to my parents and tell them that I was well.

I also wrote a letter to Tom at his APO address, which he had given me before he left the liberty ship. I was petrified when suddenly I heard the following announcement on the intercom, "Prisoner Metzroth, report to the main gate immediately."

What did I do this time? We always had a bad conscience. The First Sergeants went with me to make it official. At the gate a captain greeted us and pointed me in the direction of the offices of the Camp Commander. The sergeants wanted to know what this summons was all about, but the captain ignored them. I did not feel too well when I marched in front of him into his office. Still not speaking to me, he pointed at a chair. I sat down, glad to relieve my trembling legs. In perfect German he addressed me and slammed a piece of paper on the table.

"Where did you get an address of a U.S. soldier?"

I noticed it was the letter I had written to Tom.

"Tom was the sergeant of the guards on the ship we came over. He gave me his address so I could write him when I was in the final camp."

"You know it is forbidden to correspond with American military personnel? We are still at war with Germany." By now he spoke English with me, because he must have realized that I had written in English.

"I did not know that I was not allowed to write to a soldier. I wanted to let him know that I was all right, since he asked me to tell him."

"Well, now you know. You can write to him after the war. By the way, how did you learn to speak English?"

"In high school a little bit, but most of it I picked up being an interpreter and reading newspapers."

He calmed down considerably because he must have realized that I was not a spy or some sinister character. We ended up talking about my life and my service.

"What do you think of the war? When do you think it will be over? Who will win?"

"We will win!" I said.

He grinned, "Tell me the truth, what do you really think?"

"I must believe that we will win the war."

He still grinned. "How?"

In truth, I myself could no longer believe in a German victory since the Allies were already at Germany's borders.

"I honor your conviction," he said, "but all indications are that you are wrong. You are reading the paper. What will you do after the war?"

"I would like to come to America."

"How does this gel with you winning the war? Why would you want to come to the States if you win the war?" he asked.

By that time I was frustrated and almost in tears. I just shrugged my shoulders.

"I hope you make it to America, you don't seem to be one of the fanatics."

We talked a little more and had some friendly exchanges before he walked me to the gate.

The German sergeants were anxiously awaiting my return.

"What was this all about?"

"I had written a letter to an American soldier who had been my guard on board the ship. He had given me his address."

"Didn't you know that it is forbidden to write to the enemy?"

"How should I know? I have only been here for a few months."

I did not say more, remembering the warning I received from the captain.

A simmering bone of contention had come to a boil after the assassination attempt by German officers to kill Hitler. Shortly afterward, I think it was in the summer of 1944, all German armed forces were instructed to use the Nazi salute.

Our camp was split between those who saluted the armed forces way and those who used the Nazi salute with a raised arm. Not that we ever did a lot of saluting.

All the undercurrents were indicators of our mental state. I followed the war through the daily papers, mainly the *Stars and Stripes,* and *Time.* With the success of the Allied forces in Europe, it became more and more obvious that the German situation was disastrous and the war was coming to an end. I was torn between loyalty to my country and the daily disturbing news. What was going to happen to us after the war? The prisoners who came from the eastern part of Germany suffered most under this uncertainty. Their families tried to escape from the onrushing Soviets. Newspapers showed the endless treks of refugees streaming west. American troops had taken Trechtinghausen, and I did not have any news about my family.

Two months after the war I received a letter from my parents. My brother and my brother-in-law had survived the hostilities in Northern Germany. Our house was still standing. My father was already working again on the railroad as he had for the previous forty years. Because he had refused to join the Nazi Party, he had never been promoted to a rank higher than inspector. By the end of WWII, my father was the only railroad official who had not belonged to the Party and was, therefore, appointed superintendent of the rail yard in Bingerbrück.

Our boat had not survived the war. When the Allies had arrived at the left bank of the Rhine, the right bank was still occupied by German forces. German engineers had taken all boats across the river. To prevent the Germans from taking them for a raid on the left bank, an American mortar company received orders to destroy the boats on the other side. Our boat took a direct hit. The only parts my father could salvage were the benches and the rudder after activities had settled down.

In our camp nothing much had changed. The question on everyone's mind was, *when are we going home?* I had only been a prisoner for nine months but the old-timers were eager to see their families.

We still went to work in the tailor shop. The mountain of barracks bags became smaller and after they were done our detail joined the Warehouse 40 crew, situated near the Refer, or refrigeration building. Our job was to pick up washed clothing from the laundry plant.

Warehouse 40. Here I learned to drive the truck. On my visit, only the pillars of the foundation were standing.

After we loaded the truck, we took the laundry to W40 where women sorted it. Jim, an African-American truck driver, was trundling back and forth between the warehouse and the laundry plant. I accompanied Jim on his trips and improved my English through conversation with him. My English pronunciation did not make much progress but my *Wortschatz,* word treasure or vocabulary, expanded.

I observed how Jim shifted and handled the clutch. I asked him to let me steer while he was running the truck. He good-naturedly agreed. I enjoyed myself immensely. When the truck was parked, waiting for another load, we exchanged places and little by little I learned how to move the truck back and forth. This activity might appear trivial to Americans, but to me it felt as if I had received my driver's license.

The advantage of working at Warehouse 40 was, I did not have to wash my pants and shirts. In the rafters of the bathroom were a pot of white paint with paint thinner, a brush and two stencils, one a P and the other a W. At the end of the week, or whenever our clothes became too dirty, we picked a shirt or pant our size, took them to the bathroom and stenciled the PW on either the back of the shirt or the front of the pants' legs. We let the lettering dry and changed clothes at the end of the day. Our dirty laundry we discarded in the trash.

My ability to read articles in the American press often caused me stress. I became aware not only of the collapse of the German war effort but also learned about the Holocaust. When I saw an article and pictures of liberated concentration camps in *Time,* I could not believe what I read.

"Why do they put such stuff in the press after the war is over? They don't need any more propaganda. Germany would never commit such atrocities." I was disturbed when the older soldiers confirmed to me that such camps existed.

The war in the Pacific had not yet ended. New U.S. recruits were still coming to Camp Blanding. We watched their training. Despite the fact that we had lost the war, I felt a degree of relief that I did not have to slug through the dust and heat with backpack and rifle. But the uncertainty about our future remained.

When a new camp commander took over, he made some unpleasant changes. I don't know why he insisted on military discipline. We had to dress for reveille. As ordered, we took down the curtains we had made from flour sacks and then dyed them blue with ink. Camp personnel had to remove all the food from our kitchens and replace it with rations. I was disappointed about this commanding officer's attitude. According to the Geneva Convention, prisoners were supposed to receive the same food as the regular army. Later I learned that all prisoners of war in America received this treatment. It was beneath the esteem in which I had held the Americans. They acted illegally and in revenge.

By the end of August the war in Japan was over and all of us had to work, no more interpreters or NCOs. I was assigned to the separation center. The GIs were discharged by the thousands.

We had many POWs working in various mess halls so that we were not starving. Our work details received their rations in baskets in the morning before leaving: a slice of bologna and a handful of beans. At other times we received a hard sausage, which we called *Entmannungswurst,* or castration sausage. According to some news reports, an American politician had made the statement that all Germans should be castrated. When we brought our lunch crate and asked the cooks to fix our meal, they laughed and threw it out. We ate what the GIs ate.

Our friends in the camp who were not working awaited our return at night. Every day we smuggled some food to them in various containers. Ten eggs, broken, fit into a small mayonnaise jar. When leaving work, a prisoner put the container between his legs and brought it into the camp. A special sack could take a good amount of bacon and made its way into the camp in the same manner.

We had plenty of citrus fruit. Once in a while, for a birthday perhaps, we collected orange or grapefruit juice in gallon containers and added sugar and yeast. In ten days the concoction had developed into an alcoholic drink. *Katzenjammer,* or hangover, was the result. The First Company had also a still in the boiler room.

While working in the mess hall, life went smoothly. We did our job of washing dishes, pots and pans, and sometimes, when the kitchen was short a cook or two, we had to fill in and did it gladly. After the work was done, we sat on the steps, had a smoke and talked with the cooks.

Tranquility was shattered with the arrival of a freshly baked second lieutenant. He must have come with a contingent of new graduates of the OTC. This young guy was full of himself, which he showed in his strutting about. Of course, we were the likely targets of his Napoleon complex. According to him, there was no such thing as a break. If the dishes were done, we had to scrub the floors or weed outside the mess hall.

A friend of mine, Jupp Brock from Aachen, had a bullet lodged next to his spine and "walked funny." The bullet could not be removed without the danger of paralysis. He could not move as fast as the rest of us and became the focal point for Napoleon. Once, when the second lieutenant was after Jupp again, I tried to explain Jupp's condition to the officer. He screamed something about insubordination and stormed to the telephone to call the camp commanding officer. Shortly thereafter, a jeep with two MPs arrived. Jupp and I ended up in the pokey. The camp officer of the day told us that we were to stay for a week on bread and water for insubordination.

There was no use arguing, so we settled down. Exploring everything on the premises, we decided that conditions would not be too bad. First we took a shower. We lacked hot water, but in late summer in Florida a cold shower was refreshing. Our food consisted of a loaf of bread and the tap water, no utensils.

We could look through the bars to the next barracks and into the mess hall of the First Company. Somebody whistled and we discovered Ernst under the barracks.

"Listen, I can't stay long." he whispered. "In the john, behind the toilet, look for three loose boards, big enough for you to get through. When you are through, look for a rake with a short handle hung under the floorboards. Use the rake to erase your footprints and leave the rake under the mess hall for your return trip. Do the same when you return and hang the rake under the floorboards again. Only come when it is really dark.

"And one more thing: crawl straight across to the mess hall, not to the left, or the guards will see you from the main gate; and not to the right, or they will spot you from the guard tower on the corner. Good luck."

We had to make sure that there would be no spot checks later and so did not venture out the first evening.

We planned our food raid for the second evening. By that time we were starving. We had no electricity in the jail, therefore no lights. When it was dark, we made our little escape to food land. Being on the ground under the floor, we were sure to rake in the right direction. Because of Jupp's handicap he was the first to go across and I did the raking. After I hung the tool under the mess hall floor boards, we crawled underneath to the other side and from there under the First Company office and supply barracks. We had to wait out some traffic for a while on Main Street so that we would not attract any attention. After that, we went to our mess hall and a full supper. Also, our friends had some sandwiches ready for us to take for the next day.

"Come back in two days to take in a movie," Dammann said. At this once-a-month event, the movie was projected on the white wall of the supply barracks. We had to bring our own chairs to sit. I saw all the Road Pictures during my stay and liked Bob Hope better than Bing Crosby.

Returning to the jail from our outing was just as uneventful. Our sandwiches had to be stored behind the john. The next day was boring and we entertained ourselves by making little marbles out of bread and water. We dried them in the sun and could use them the next day.

After a week we were released with an admonishment to our first sergeants to keep us in check.

All in all, the time as a POW was boring. I was not the most industrious person. The best description of me would be to call me Beatle Bailey. I was young, without guidance, and lazy. German teachers gave lectures on various subjects but I would rather play Ping-Pong, Volleyball, or sleep. My favorite snacks were Moon Pies and Orange Nehi. We were paid in script, $1.00 per working day. Once a month we received a little perforated pad in various denominations such as 1 cent, 5 cents, dimes, quarters and $1.00s. There was not much we could buy in the PX. By the time of my repatriation I had saved over one hundred dollars.

As time went by, and the year 1945 came to an end, we were getting more and more anxious to go home. Germany had been divided into four Zones of Occupation: the American Zone, the

British Zone, the Soviet Zone and, of course, the zone of the *victorious* French. In the spring of 1946 it became evident that repatriation proceedings had started. We were to be discharged by zones. Ernst left first, going home to the British zone; then the American zone and after that the Russian zone shipped out.

We were still waiting to be sent home to the French zone. Little did we know that previously released German POWs were handed over to the French authorities and retaken prisoners. All their possessions were confiscated. Some of these prisoners were pressed into the French Foreign Legion and shipped to Vietnam. At that time the French were still trying to hold on to their colonies. Many Germans ended up later as prisoners of the Vietcong and, since the Vietcong were closely associated with the Soviet Union, these Germans were handed over to the Russians. To obtain some positive press coverage in the world, the Russians released these men to West Germany, even though the Soviets were still holding thousands of German prisoners from WWII.

Hubert and I were from the areas in the French zone. Finally, our day came in February 1946. We were shipped to Camp Shanks in New York State. After our confinement in Florida the change of climate was a chock. But a greater blow was in store for us.

At Camp Shanks we underwent additional interviews and repeated the march-by with raised arms that we had passed fifteen months earlier in Hampton Roads.

After a week in Camp Shanks we heard this announcement, "You will be loaded on a troop ship and transported back to Germany." We would be home for Easter! What elation. Who cares what life will be in Germany when we get there. Just to get home. I had left in 1943 when I was sixteen years old and now it was 1946. In these three years the world had changed so much.

Embarkation on the Hudson River followed two days later. The accommodations on board the ship were considerably better than on a Liberty ship: five bunks on top of each other to sleep in; a regular mess hall to take our meals. We were a happy bunch. As soon as we were on board, the ship left on a slow trip down the Hudson. The prisoners followed the announcement for the first serving immediately. But I stayed on deck, hungry or not, I had to see New York City and the Statue of Liberty in the harbor. There were no more guards. A member of the crew approached me.

"Didn't you hear the mess call?"

"Yes, I did, but I want to see New York City. I might never come back to see it, so it is worth going hungry for an evening."

The sight was overpowering, especially the sea of lights in the city and the reflection of the setting sun in the windows. I marveled at this picture of wealth and peace.

The vessel took up speed and plowed through the harbor and by the Statue of Liberty. It was an all-expense paid cruise.

CRUISING THE BRITISH ISLES

The crossing was uneventful. Every morning a posted chart showed us how our position point was slowly inching across the Atlantic. We were nearing Europe and figured we might be in the English Channel by the next day.

Waking up that morning, I dashed to the chart to check our progress. There is something wrong with this chart. We are not in the Channel but in the Irish Sea, between Ireland and England, and we are heading north.

The announcement over the intercom shocked us all, "We will be docking in the harbor of Liverpool by evening. You will be loaded on a train to reach your next destination."

"Maybe they are sending us to Dover and from there across the Channel by ferry to Germany," I said, clinging desperately to this belief. Any other explanation for disembarkation in England was too horrible to be true.

We boarded the train in darkness and left the station soon afterward. Not having any means to determine in which direction we were heading, we settled down to sleep.

In the morning, we woke to a snow-covered landscape. This can't be Dover. There was no snow in Liverpool, and Dover is even further south than Liverpool. Where are we? When the train stopped, the sign of the station read Ayrshire. Where is Ayrshire? British MPs herded us onto trucks; crushed, we drove through a dismal landscape. What is happening to us? Are we not headed to Dover to be discharged? The situation was confusing.

A short ride later, we arrived at a camp. Dingy tarpaper-covered barracks, gloomy fellow prisoners, and loud dialog over the intercom greeted us. The NCOs gave us our barracks assignments. Upon entering the wooden structures we did not receive any greeting, just gestures where our bunks were: double bunks with straw-filled mattresses. No one smiled. Again, Hubert was in another barracks.

Prisoner in Scotland in 1946.

Before long, a sergeant in charge called us out. "You are now prisoners of the Crown. You will receive new POW numbers. All your khakis are to be turned in and exchanged for British POW clothes. You will be issued mess kits, consisting of a tin bowl, fork, spoon, and a cup. You will bring them later to the mess hall when you are called out. Dismissed."

We were in a daze. What had happened? What about the promise by the American officer that we would be home by Easter?

I was desperate. *Maybe Hubert has the answer.* But Hubert was just as baffled. Being an old hand at solving problems, he expressed his thought.

"Did you see the arm patches the guys at the gate and the sergeants have? It says *Austria* on them. These bastards are turncoats. They were all gung-ho when the war was in our favor, and now that all is lost, they want to be victims."

"That explains their arrogant behavior," I said.

With all our troubles we had to cope with these characters, too. "But why are the other prisoners so standoffish with us?"

"I think they are envious. They had been in England for the duration and dislike us because they think we had a better time in the States. That is the only explanation I have."

As usual, Hubert was right.

The constant chatter on the intercom was nerve-wracking. I realized that the proceedings at the Nuremberg Trials were broadcast to us all day long. With the broken promise of our return home and the extension of our POW time, we were demoralized already. Was the purpose of the broadcasts to punish us for Nazi crimes? Self-involved, none of us paid any attention to the messages.

The only redeeming value of this camp, located in a hilly cow pasture, was that we were allowed to go outside the perimeter. For the first time in two years we could go outside without any guards.

Fortunately, after a week or two, our stay in this pool of intrigues came to an end. We were loaded on trucks and left. The ride took us across northern Scotland, from the west coast to the east coast. A town called Montrose was to be our home. The camp was located on Rosemont, an estate. This time our shelters were corrugated metal Nissen huts without heat, each housing about fifty men. In the morning we scraped frost from the walls. A few minutes of Florida heat would have been welcome. The "natives" were friendly.

We had received our British uniforms in the previous camp; the same as those of the British army, with one exception: ours were died dark blue. The back of our jackets featured a maroon patch, about 12"x12", sewn into a square hole. During the winter months, I was happy to still have my American woolen overcoat.

We could not comprehend our situation. Still in shock over the deception, we managed to adjust to current conditions.

An extensive park, now filled with Nissen huts, surrounded the estate of Rosemont and its large mansion. The Allies probably had a base here during the war. We prisoners occupied only three of the huts.

After a week at the camp, we received our work detail assignments. Lorries picked us up in the morning and took us to work in the farm fields. The mess had prepared sandwiches for our lunch and stored them in a box. With the box came a square tin can. Every one of us received a spoon of dried tea. At lunchtime, we started a fire in the field or the farmyard to heat water for the tea in the tin can.

We categorized the farmers as milk or no-milk farmers. Did they supply us with milk for our tea, or not? We worked harder for the milk farmers' small gesture.

At the end of every week we collected one shilling per workday. There was no more script. We needed to get used to the strange money: farthing, halfpenny, penny, sixpence, and shilling.

While the weather was still too cold for planting, the farmer sent us to a field right at the coast. I remember the wind blowing fiercely from the water, making the air dank and cold. We were confronted with an endless berm, which turned out to be a mite, containing potatoes harvested in the previous fall. To open the mite, we first removed the earth and then the straw cover to reach the taters, which we sorted and bagged with numb hands.

In the fall we had to harvest potatoes again. A tractor pulled the harvester, laying the potatoes in neat rows. Each prisoner had a certain length of row to pick clean. Naturally the tractor operator tried to speed up the harvest, and we had to work hard to keep up with the tempo. It did not take us long to observe that the chain of the harvester jumped the wheels when struck by a larger rock. Then the tractor operator had to stop to reinstall the chain. When the operator tried to speed up again, and he was not looking, a designated thrower pitched a rock into the works and the repair started all over again. We tried to tell him that he was going too fast for the machinery. He finally slowed down.

On another work detail, we went to a field where grain was stored in stacks. Our job was to feed the threshing machine. Assigned to a Scottish threshing crew, we moved with them from field to field. Their approach to the task was interesting.

First, we worked the stack down to a height of about three feet. Then we erected a chicken wire fence around it to keep the mice and rats, which occupied the stack over the winter, from escaping. The crew always brought two or three ratter dogs along. As we reduced the layers of straw, the mice and rats tried to escape but were kept inside the fenced-in area and the ratters went to work. These little dogs grabbed the rodents by the head and shook them, thus killing the pests, often as many as twenty-five per stack.

We liked to work with the crew. Every noon an old Rolls taxi appeared. The driver had picked up an insulated container with Scotch broth from a restaurant. We appreciated the Scottish crew's empathy and enjoyed the piping hot soup as a nice addition to our sandwich and tea. The men got their money's worth out of us.

The rumor mill is always active in a POW camp, "Prisoners with injuries or inability to do a day's work will be shipped home." Soon, the rumor became reality. Everybody with a complaint was to report to the camp medic. He in turn made appointments with a physician. Hubert had a trick elbow, which he could activate at will. I don't know how he did it, but he was shipped home.

I have a scar on the left lower arm and thought to try my luck with the doctor. I reported to the medic and received an appointment. I told the physician, "It hurts with strenuous work." He examined the arm and told me that it could not be so bad.

"But it hurts when I strain it," I re-emphasized.

"I tell you what. Here's a handkerchief, go in the corner and cry. You are fit to work."

I kept the handkerchief and left.

Around this time, the repatriation quotas were announced. Those who had been taken prisoner in the earlier years were to go home first. The verdict I received was: two more years! I was at the end of my rope. In all my life I had never been so down as I was at that time. It was late spring 1946 and, according to the schedule, I would not be home before spring 1948. If I had been a criminal and had been sentenced to two years, I would have understood. But this…the unfairness was incomprehensible. The news must have been just as bad for my parents when I wrote them about it.

Hubert had left; soon I received a card from him saying he was getting married. Good luck to him.

I had to get on with my life. We were all on edge. I had gotten into a fight with a man twice my size. Herbert May stepped in and saved my hide.

Herbert had been a submariner whose sub had been sunk in May 1944 by a Polish destroyer, which had escaped to England in 1939. The Polish sailors machine-gunned the U-Boot survivors in the water. Herbert was wounded in the knee. He never forgave the Poles their violation of international law at sea, and often retold his experience. Being from Breslau, which had become Polish territory after the war, did not help soothe Herbert's anger. His father had been a skipper on the Oder River, and Herbert served as a mate. As a POW, Herbert worked in the bush in Canada for two years before being sold into slavery, like us.

In Scotland, Herbert kept his eyes on me, "Keep your big mouth shut and stay out of fights."

We had developed a sideline for additional income in Montrose. As members of the threshing crew we had to cut the strings that were holding the bales together. Instead of throwing the ties away, we saved the strings. Two guys in the camp double-braided them and made a long rope. They arranged this rope and, on edge, sewed it into soles for slippers. The tops were finished with remnants of material so that feet could slip into the created footwear. I bought these slippers for two shillings a pair. During work breaks, I sold them to civilians house to house for three shillings. We could not make them fast enough. By this time we were free to go almost anywhere.

The British people were friendly beyond belief. We did not encounter animosity. They had been through hell throughout the war but, being fair-minded, they did not hold it against us.

Once, we were indentured to a gardener of a large hospital. The hospital was surrounded by many acres of land on which the administration grew vegetables, such as long rows of freshly planted carrots and leeks. We had to thin out the carrots and keep them weed free. When the vegetables matured, we supplemented our lunches with the tender, small carrots and leeks. After a *leeky* lunch we turned into a smelly bunch; but since we were among each other, nobody but innocent bystanders turned their noses.

Before another unpleasant winter in northern Scotland, we moved approximately 325 miles south to an Air Force base near Cheltenham, Gloucestershire. Our camp was close to a small village, Churchdown. All of the prisoners had jobs at the air base. To get to work, we used the bicycles issued to us. We could also use them for rides in the countryside. Since we did not have restrictions, I explored the surroundings on weekends.

On one of my excursions I met Doris, a nineteen-year-old pretty girl. I first spoke to her in an old cemetery. From then on we made trips on our bikes together. I was smitten, or more accurately, we were smitten.

An old-timer in my barracks called me aside and warned me about the birds and the bees, when he found out I dated a girl. I appreciated his concern.

The airfield in Cheltenham gradually changed from an active airport to an MP training center. Many officers' quarters were dismantled. We had to store all mattresses in a big warehouse, the right job for me: I could take it easy between deliveries by truck. But this time luck deserted me. I developed an allergy from the mattress dust, resulting in severe headaches; so I volunteered for the gardener job in fresh air. Raking, and painting everything white that did not move, kept me occupied.

The buildings marked for demolition had beautiful blue cotton curtains inside, which were also to be stored in the warehouse but ended up in our camp as well. One curtain had enough material to make a pair of leisure pants. For two curtains, our tailor made a pair of pants for me and kept the other pair to sell. I took my pants with me when I was discharged and still had them, when I emigrated to the States.

The air base housed a kennel with about twenty German Shepherds. They were being trained for the air police. Herbert had a job cleaning the kennels and cutting meat for the dogs. His boss was a cute MP corporal. They spent a lot of time in the freezer together. Fraternization was in full bloom. When he introduced me to her, she said that she had a girl friend, a sergeant, no less.

"Do you want to meet her?" I declined. I was in love with Doris.

The next transfer brought us to the east again: to Tonbridge in Kent. I missed Doris terribly. We did write to each other. I don't know how we thought we would meet again. We simply did not want to think far ahead.

Our group arrived in Tonbridge in the fall of 1947 just before harvest time. Farmers still had some stacks of grain in the barns from the previous year. These remainders had to be threshed before the new harvest came in. Again, our crew took on this task.

"Imagine the infestation of mice and rats after a year!" I said to my buddy.

The ratters killed the rodents but their refuse contaminated the dust associated with threshing. After two days, I developed a severe respiratory infection, probably from mice feces, and ended up in the hospital on the critical list. I was semi-conscious for two days.

At my discharge the doctor said. "You are lucky, you almost didn't make it."

Lucky enough to celebrate my twenty-first birthday.

The harvest was in full swing after my return from the hospital. My next assignment sent me to a detail bringing in hay. One day, while waiting for our truck to take us back to the camp, I picked blackberries and missed the truck. Since I did not want to get into trouble, I hiked back to the farm where I asked the farmer's wife, "Could I possibly get a ride back to the camp?"

"Yes, but first you will have supper with us. We will call the camp and let them know you are here, and then we will take you back as soon as we have eaten," she said.

We spent a nice evening together, had a glass of wine and enjoyed good conversation. Before dark, they took me back to the camp.

My six shillings a week allowed me to save some money and still go out on the town for the weekend. On Sundays, we went to the movies for one shilling. To our amazement, people smoked in the theater. Before every movie, we listened to the national anthem, "God save the King." After the film, our next stop was at a Fish-and-Chips place. For a shilling and a half we received a good portion of Fish and Chips, wrapped in newspaper. On the way back to the camp, two shillings bought us a cup of tea and a slice of cake at a stand. So, for four and half shillings we had a good time on a Sunday afternoon.

We spent the Christmas holidays of 1947 still in Tonbridge. On Boxing Day we played the local soccer team and won. Two friends of mine and I were invited to the home of Mr. and Mrs. S. Sudds, 225 Beaver Lane, Ashford, Kent, after the game. I still have a snapshot of Mrs. Sudds with her Golden Retriever puppies. On the back of the picture she had written her address. Mrs. Sudds served a wonderful Christmas dinner. I will always remember the generosity and friendliness of the English people.

Every month some of our group were repatriated according to plan. I had just a few more months to wait before I could at last go home after another transfer: to Dover, Kent, my last camp.

Actually, it was a former Navy prison on the right cliff when looking at Dover from the sea. There we lived in a regular prison building with cells and a big wall surrounding the installation. Four men shared a two-men cell. In the morning, two had to stay in the bunks so that the other two could dress.

In my first detail in Dover I met Christmann from Assmannhausen; together we exchanged memories of our hometowns. We worked in construction, laying curbstones for a new development not far from the prison. During my time in Britain, I must have performed almost any kind of menial labor.

My last job, shortly before my repatriation, sent me to Dover Castle. From its elevated position I could overlook the whole town and also could see the French coast on the horizon.

The keeper of the castle, an elderly gentleman, pointed me to the terrace. "Clean up the flowerbeds, remove all weeds, and prepare the beds for planting," he said.

On the terrace I found a wide, grassy area with the neglected, overgrown flowerbeds barely distinguishable from the lawn. I became depressed at the sight. *Where to begin?*

I worked furiously: weeding and turning the soil for hours.

At the end of the day the castle's keeper came to see me.

"Time to go 'home'. You did a splendid job."

He had probably expected that I loafed all day. Full of praise, he shook my hand. "Keep up the good work and you will go far in life."

GOING HOME

The day for my departure from England had arrived. I said goodbye to my friend, Christmann, and promised him to look up his parents when I got home.

A lorry took a group of us, about forty to fifty, to the railroad station where we boarded a local train to Charring Cross Station in London, then changing to another, which took us to Harwich. Massive dark clouds looked foreboding when we embarked a ferry for Hoek van Holland in the Netherlands. Heavy rain and cold, salty spray pelted the deck in the stormy night crossing. Many of us went below and stayed in the warmer corridors. I sat on my duffel bag on deck in a protected corner: I did not want to miss anything. The vessel pounded through the waves, a typical North Sea crossing. Soon the guys who had gone below came on deck to pay tribute to King Neptune. I had my cozy spot behind a lifeboat and was not seasick because I had fresh air.

We landed in the Netherlands in the morning. After transport to the railroad station, we climbed aboard a reserved car for returning POWs. These special cars were routinely attached to trains leaving for Germany because of the continuous flow of POWs coming out of England.

The trip to Münsterlager, an English repatriation camp in Germany for returning German prisoners, took us through territory I had not seen for five years. Soon after we left the Dutch station, we crossed the border: I was in Germany. As a prisoner, I felt a strange awareness of being outside the present surroundings. I was segregated, not so much physically, but emotionally, and positioned myself not in the focal area, but always at the fringe. I needed time, even after I returned, to overcome this feeling of being a second-rate person. The four years of my imprisonment are forever marked in my mind.

I had left in the spring of 1944 as a blond-haired youngster and returned in 1948 as a young man with dark brown hair. I had grown and gained weight. My disposition had mellowed considerably. On the day of my return to Germany I was elated.

How will my family have changed? Just as the war left its marks on the landscape and the buildings, it certainly affected the people. Troops fighting to defend their country and others to conquer it heaped hardships and wounds on the population.

The processing in Münsterlager was efficient and fast, by now routine. My discharge papers had to be signed by a French officer in a French repatriation camp. Because the French had such a bad record in discharging POWs, a British officer accompanied our group to Bretzenheim in the French Zone. He was to make sure that the French did not take us prisoners again. This officer stayed until the last one of us left the camp for home.

On the way from Münsterlager to the French camp, our train had to pass the switching station of Bingerbrück. My father worked there. He was aware of our passing through the station and was waiting for me. We were rolling right through and I was looking through the window on the right side of the train. Nearly through the station, I thought I heard my name called, "RUPERTUS", on the other side of the train. I rushed to the other window, and there was my father running next to our train, trying to keep up with us. I screamed and he waived. And then we had passed the station.

Rupertus is my baptized name. Nobody but our priest or teacher ever called me by the name. Maybe my mother, when she wanted to emphasize her directions to me.

Later I asked my father why he had shouted Rupertus, since he usually called me Bert.

"I never did," he said.

So, who did? I cannot explain it.

86

Think for Yourself

We had arrived in Bretzenheim at the beginning of a big weekend, Mardi Gras. Consequently, the French CO did not come into camp until Ash Wednesday. Those Frenchies never change.

Midmorning on Ash Wednesday we were finally released. What an odd feeling: I did not belong to any work detail. I did not have to go to roll call. After six years I was free. Almost one third of my life had been spent with those in authority telling me what I had to do, first in the German service, then as a POW.

I shouldered my duffel bag and headed for the railroad station. Returning German veterans did not have to pay for the ticket. A local train brought us to the junction Bingerbrück. Eagerly looking out the window, I was shocked by the devastation: this junction had vanished. There were no buildings left standing. A few shacks set up for the administration was all I could see nearly three years after the war. The antiaircraft tower, where I had been stationed as a Luftwaffenhelfer, was flattened. The crew must have died. All the underpasses leading to the various platforms had collapsed at this station.

In Bingerbrück I had to change trains and arrived at the time of day when the commuting students of the high school I had attended, came to the station for their trip home. These kids were young and totally *undisciplined.* They did the kidding and loud-mouthing we used to do, but now they struck me as ridiculous. Boy, was I old.

Some of the students' faces showed features of their parents, familiar to me. The young people, however, certainly did not know this strange-looking man in his oversized American army overcoat and light blue Canadian prisoner cap with a bright red top. Herbert had given it to me before he went home.

At last the train rolled into the station. The doors had no windows, just plywood inserts with little peepholes in the middle.

Since my hometown was only five miles north of Bingerbrück, I did not settle down in the train but stayed at the door to see some of the scenery.

Germania, the National Monument, was still at the top of the mountain above the right bank of the Rhine. The Mouse Tower still guarded the rapids of the *Binger Loch.* Soon Assmannshausen came into view with its mountainsides of vineyards and the rows of luxury hotels untouched by war. The *Leisten,* so called because it had the form of a shoe last, is a rock in the middle of the river. It had not moved. I had lost a paddle there years ago. Then, on our side of the river, the first of our three local castles came into view, and shortly thereafter our cemetery with the eight-hundred-year-old *Klemenskapelle,* a church dedicated to St. Clemens, the patron of sailors on the Rhine river. Thank God, it was not touched, and all my ancestors buried around it were still there and greeted me.

When the train arrived at the station, I read the sign: Trechtingshausen. I had not seen it for so many years. On the platform I hesitated: *Was I really back home?* Finally I emerged from the underpass that brought me to the exit. Hooting, hollering and screaming startled me. *What was going on?* When I came closer, I noticed the crowd was screaming for me. On this day they had met every train that came from Bingerbrück. Now they saw me. Adam Tabarelli, one of my close friends, rushed toward me, greeting me with tears in his eyes. He took my duffel bag to carry it for me. Adam still had the big scar on his forehead. *Why wouldn't he?* He incurred it while participating in some horseplay with our gang.

Off we went in a triumphal procession from the railroad station towards my parents' house, *Unterstrasse 140a.*

We had to go from one end of the village through the settlement, to the other end. As it happens in a small place, the news spread faster than a man can walk. Doors and windows opened and faces I had known seemed to be changed, not exactly old but different. Everybody wanted to participate in the joy of my return. I was not the first POW to come home, many had come before me and many would still have to come after me. The country was slowly adjusting to peace.

Nearing Nr.140a my buddies toned down their continuous questions. Below the front door, Adam called out, "*Fra Metzerod, de Berdus is do,"* or Mrs. Metzroth, Bert is here. I heard a commotion inside. Adam gave me my duffel bag and pushed me toward the stairs leading to the entrance. Slowly my buddies drifted away while I rushed up the first section of the familiar stairs in two leaps. Memories flashed through my mind.

One winter morning an icy patch had sent me flying down these stairs with my nose hitting a flowerpot. An excuse not to have to go to church.

The last stairs I took slower in anticipation of what was to come. There was the old brass nameplate my father used to polish every Saturday; the little window my mother used to open and see who was at the door. And this door now opened.

My mother hugged me first, then my sister and behind them my father. I don't recall what we said as I was engulfed in a wave of joy.

When we stepped back to look at each other, I noticed that wrinkles in their faces had deepened. Papa's short hair met his temples from the back, leaving the top of his head bald. Mutter's happiness at having her youngest home spread across her face and shone from her sky-blue, tear-filled eyes. Wearing her flowered apron, Ina had run from the kitchen to greet me. *"Na, endlich,"* she said, or well, finally!

Then my mother asked the eternal, universal questions on mothers' minds when they greet their sons, *"Hosche Hunger, wilsche was esse?"* Are you hungry, do you want to eat?

My father held back until the female exuberance had somewhat abated. In his embrace he said: *"Jetschd bische deham, mei Bub."* Now you are home, son.

A little boy stood blending into the background, my nephew who had been born shortly before I left and to whom I was godfather.

"Bisch du de Pätter?" Are you my godfather?

"Jo, un du bischd de Reiner?" Yes, and you are Reiner?

This all took place in the entrance corridor. Eventually my father said,

"Dann komm dochemo ne renn." Let's go inside.

In the living room he looked at me and exclaimed, *"Mensch, du bischd awer groswor."* Man, you really have grown.

My grandmother, or Oma, small and fragile, could finally come to ask me, *"Gell, mei bede hot geholf?"* I am sure my prayers helped, didn't they?

Now my mother wanted to scurry into the kitchen to set the table.

"Mother, I can wait a little longer. Let me give you the presents I brought for all of you." I took my duffel bag, actually a large sea bag with straps to carry like a rucksack, and unpacked the gifts.

"Is Santa a little late or very early?" Ina asked.

Food was still rationed in Germany and I was happy to help my family with coffee, tea and cans of meat.

The day of my homecoming passed so quickly. In the evening, Karl and my brother-in-law, Walter, came home from work. After dinner, Papa uncorked his best *Rhein-Wein* for our family's celebration. We caught up with many events, which had happened to each of us during our separation. We went to bed in the early morning hours. *This time no taps.*

The next morning I woke up to the almost forgotten sounds of my childhood. A very busy railroad line about one hundred yards from our house reminded me of the shortcut across the tracks to the swimming hole in the Rhine. I heard the waters rushing by the red buoy, which I could see from my window. It took a while for me to get oriented and to realize my situation: I was home! In the house, everyone was quiet.

What now? What should I do first? I mean what should I do? Nobody tells me anything anymore! I have to help my father as well as I can. But what about the future? I think I will talk to Karl.

I got up and started to rummage through my duffel for some clothes. It was still spring and rather cool. The only warm stuff I had was POW outfits and they were rather dirty since we had been underway for quite a while and did not have a chance to wash them. My old clothes, which I found in my closet did not fit me anymore. So, unfortunately, I had to wear a POW uniform again.

Most older returning vets had no problems with outgrown clothes when they came home.

I showed up late for breakfast the first morning. *Oma, Mutter,* or mother, and Ina greeted me cheerfully, ready to spoil me. Ina and her husband had moved into the second floor of my parent's house because of the housing shortage. I was glad that Ina was available for counseling.

"Was soll ich dann jetz mache?" I asked my sister. What should I do now?

"Garnix, komm erschtemo zu der." Get your bearing first, she said. *"Gemo bei de Kall. Der werder schun sahn wies is."* Check with your brother, Karl, he will let you in on things. *"Waasche wo der jetz wohnt?"* Do you know where he lives now?

"Na, awer er hot mer gesaht es is uff de Schossee gejeiwwer funde Fina, sei Schwiermudder." No, but he told me he lives on Main Street across from Fina, his mother-in-law's store.

After breakfast I was on the way to see my brother. It took me a while to get there. The neighbors had to say hello and wanted their questions answered. Slowly I worked my way through the welcomers. Some girls caught my attention, but I figured to first get the whole picture of my hometown and its people after my years of absence.

I finally made it to Main Street and found my brother's apartment. Karl was cleaning up his garage.

"Gude," he said with a grin, good morning. *Hoschenix besseres ahnseziehe?"* Don't you have anything better to wear?

"Ich honn alles ausgewax." I outgrew everything.

Karl called to his wife in their upstairs apartment, above the garage,

"Gisela, kommdochemo ne runner, der Berdus is do." Gisela, come down, Bert is here.

My brother had married after he was released as a POW in the summer of 1945. Unfortunately, his wife was a girl I had dated for a while, but had broken up with before I was drafted. I did not care for her any longer but could not do anything about her being my sister-in-law (The marriage broke up a few years later.). My brother and I were close, but he was now a married man and had obligations, such as going to work and other unpleasant things I tried to stay away from.

Gisela and I greeted each other reservedly. For the time being she acted in a civil manner. Little did I know that she had her plans already. My brother was so happy to see me again. We went upstairs and, as was the custom, he opened a bottle of wine.

Then Karl became serious.

"The French are on the prowl, actually have been for some time. The *Sûreté*, the French Secret Service, is keeping an eye on our village again."

I was intrigued by the story he told me.

There had been an underground railroad through which German prisoners, escaped from the French camps, were channeled to our area.

Because Trechtingshausen was the only village in our area along the Rhine with vineyards on both sides of the river, a whole fleet of private boats was needed to transport the vintners across to work. The right bank of the river was in the American Zone of Occupation and a pass was required for the locals to go across the river. Many German prisoners of the French military, who wanted to escape to the British or the American zone, soon learned about this possible escape route through the underground grapevine. The escapees came at night and knocked on any door in the village; they were guided to the men with boats who took them over to freedom.

Some girls fraternized with the *Kakerlacken,* cockroaches, as the French were called here. To be girlfriends with the British or the American troops was accepted, but associating with the French was taboo. So the girls could have been informers as well. Stoolpigeons gradually infiltrated the nest and arrests took place.

French authorities slowly accumulated a list of men who had assisted POWs on their way to freedom. One night the secret service rounded them up and threw them all in jail. After weeks without court proceedings, two men were released because they were dying. An old man at the age of eighty and a boy of sixteen had developed pneumonia in the dank cellars of the prison and were weakened by the interrogator's beatings. Both men died a few days later.

My brother was lucky that he was not arrested. Because our father had lost his boat in the war and did not have a new one yet, he and Karl were not proven to have participated.

And I thought the war was over.

Later, Karl had built a new boat from sheet metal.

"Wo hosche dann des Blech kried?" From where did you get the sheet metal?

"Das hemmer fun de Kackerlacke geklaut," We snitched it from the French.

"Wie hosche dann das ahngestellt?" How did you manage that?

Karl told me the story of the snitch.

My brother worked at the switching yard of Bingerbrück. Once a week a shipment of reparation sheet metal came through from the industry in the Ruhr valley.

"The sheet metal had been loaded on flat cars," Karl said. "So my buddies and I had a plan. When the next shipment arrived, we declared that a wagon was running hot with faulty bearings. Then we sidelined this wagon 'to be repaired.' The sideline track was next to a steep incline leading to the *Leinpfad,"* or line path, formerly used by teams of horses to assist ships by pulling them upstream. Karl continued, "We removed the retaining rungs of the wagon on the side facing the river. Now some sheets slid down the embankment; I reserved four sheets for myself. Afterwards we replaced the rungs, declared the wagon repaired and sent the remaining load on its way to France."

In the morning after their night activity, my brother, with the help of his co-workers, loaded his sheets on a hidden cart and transported the loot to our local blacksmith. For a price of one sheet, he was allowed to build the boat from the remaining sheets with the blacksmith's tools at his shop.

There were still hard times in Germany. The money was worthless; people could buy few things with it. Food was still rationed and the only place to obtain anything worthwhile was on the black market.

Into this climate I, the former prisoner of war, found myself released. Abroad I had envisioned personal freedom but did not know about the shortages of food, clothing and other essentials the German population tried to supplement daily.

My brother Karl at the control of the emergency locomotive.

The boat my brother built from French sheet metal.
On the second forward bench is the hole into which the mast
was stepped.

SUSPENDED

I felt I was floating in mid-air. After coming home I had the sense of still being the sixteen-year old who had just left. My parents gave me all the space I needed for readjustment. Today I am just as confused about those days as I was then. I have no coherent memory about that time and can only recall episodes that occurred, but not in sequence.

Totally uprooted from any awareness of events with which I had dealt before, I needed to make a decision about my future and what I wanted out of life. Since January 1943 I had made only one choice of my own: to volunteer for the Airborne troops. In all other situations I could always blame circumstances for my fate. Two years in the military and four years as a POW rarely allowed me to think for myself, as my father had always encouraged me to do. It must have been awful for him to watch me struggle after my return home, yet he never said a critical word.

The doors to education were virtually closed to me. I would have to start at twenty-two years of age where I had left off at sixteen. Educational courses for returning veterans offered right after the war were discontinued and compelled us latecomers to find other resources.

At first, I buried myself in work. There was enough to do in my father's gardens and vineyards. I was accepted by the men who had been through the wringer as I had been. They greeted me with friendly and understanding nods. In general, nobody talked about his ordeals, but most had a long story to tell. Sometimes, at rounds in the tavern, one would start talking about an incident and we listened. We knew he had to tell somebody. Many of the old-timers who had been in the service for a long time and had reached the rank of sergeant were penalized by the new government for being militarists and were forced to take menial jobs.

We veterans still felt a bond forged through combat experience, unspoken but real.

One short incident describes our ties. At a dance, a butcher's son who had been able to avoid the service tried to horn in on my date, Ruth. He became rather belligerent when Ruth and I ignored him. Two of my veteran buddies made a sharp remark to him and he disappeared with the sausages he had brought to impress a girl.

We lived it up during this time of despair. People could not buy anything worthwhile. The only means for bartering we had was wine. Going to a dance we brought our own bottle of wine and two German marks for the band. In the summer, short pants and a white shirt was the dress of the night.

For work, Karl gave me overalls to wear, and short pants and some shirts for leisure. Mutter worked on my Luftwaffenhelfer uniform to change it into a civilian jacket. The war had reduced many people to poverty. They did not care what a person wore. I had some dollars saved from my time in the States and cashed them in for some worthless German marks to have pocket money.

Karl and I got along well until his wife started to make trouble. Gisela tried to move in on me; when she did not succeed she told my brother I had pursued her. Sadly enough my brother believed her. For decades Karl and I did not speak to each other. Only after he was divorced could we communicate again and that was too late; he died shortly afterwards.

I drifted into a life of ease. It was not hard to make money on the black market. In our area, wine was easy to obtain but foodstuffs were scarce. Lorenz, called Lor, was a friend several years older than I. He devised a plan to travel to the Ruhr valley, an area rich in coal mines and industry. There we could barter for herrings, which were shipped in because the miners as well as workers employed by steel mills received more food rations and were eager to trade some food for wine.

Lor and I collected fifteen bottles of wine each and took the train north into the Ruhr valley. A fish merchant traded us three herrings per bottle. With a barrel of fish between the two of us, we returned riding on the running boards of the train because the compartments were thoroughly overcrowded. In our village we could exchange one fish for a bottle of wine. That left us with two herrings for profit. After a few trips we were able to have enough money for a down payment on a surplus jeep and trailer.

Now we were in business. Real money could be made with firewood. More accurately, with firewood reserved for the French as reparation cost. Every German family was allotted one cord for the coming winter, which was pitifully little. The German foresters were compelled to cut hundreds of cords for the French occupation forces, clearing acres of beautiful stands of beech trees. One trip per day into the forest with the jeep was enough to pay off the loan for the jeep and enough to live well, and live well we did.

Lor was a rogue. He walked with a slight limp because of a bum knee incurred in the service. But limping had the same effect as an eye patch on a pirate. He was the Tyron Power type in looks and lived accordingly. I was a fast learner.

Barter business thrived since the German Mark was not worth much. A forest restaurant needed sand for building an addition. We delivered sand to the construction site and returned with French or "frog" wood, which kept us financially stable. The restaurant owner had a standing tab for us for food and drink. We could never drink our quota and engaged female help. Seldom were we without female companions during this time.

I remember I went to a dance in Bingen and met some of my classmates. One, who had been able to avoid the service, gave me a hard time by pointing out his accomplishments against mine. He had a beautiful wife with him but could not dance too well. I helped him out and danced with her several times. They left earlier than I did. By the time I was ready to go home she was standing at the railroad station waiting for me. What now? In the past Lor always knew what to do. So Katie and I went to his apartment. It took a while to rouse him from his sleep.

"Lor, get up and sleep on your parent's couch!"

"What the hell are you talking about?"

When he saw Katie, he grumbled, picked up his clothes and left.

"You owe me one, Berdes."

Katie left early in the morning on the train; I never saw her again, neither did my classmate. His law degree did not help him much in his marriage. I felt a little vindicated. The doubt about my future, however, was still gnawing at me.

On another day Lor came and said, "Berdes, I have a lead on a pig for a hundred German marks and some bottles of wine."

"When are we going?"

"Tomorrow night. First, I have to line up a butcher who will slaughter the pig."

Off we went with jeep and trailer into the Hunsrück mountains the next evening. Loading the pig on the trailer was not much of a problem, but the animal would not lie down. We zigzagged all across the road. The pig was rolling from one side of the trailer to the other, but as soon as we straightened out, it was up again. We did not think of tying its feet together so the pig could not get up.

Another problem arose when we had to cross the Nahe River over the Drusus bridge, the same one Roman legions used to march over. All traffic went across this bridge to enter Bingen. At the center of the bridge, a policeman was checking for contraband. We veered from side to side, but the critter did not lie down, on the contrary, it voiced its displeasure adamantly. When we passed the policeman he saw our cargo but did not stop us.

After unloading the pig into the butcher shop we heard a knock on the door. The cop. Two sausages pacified him; after that, the slaughter and the dividing went on without a hitch.

I was looking forward to autumn when I could work full-time for my father; the harvest of grapes was approaching. Local authorities controlled the beginning of this harvest. To attain the best quality for the wine, we could not pick the grapes before they reached the set sugar content. The reputation of the region's wine is always at stake. Every wine-producing area strives to maintain its hard-earned good name.

My father and many of Trechtingshausen's vintners owned vineyards on both banks of the Rhine. They ferried across the river in their *Nachen* to tend to their vines, an almost year-long undertaking.

The preparations for the harvest began two to three days before the actual grape picking. We loaded the boats with wooden vats, carts, smaller wooden tubs, and the *Legels*. Men carried one of these containers on their backs to collect the grapes. Two days before the harvest we rowed the top-heavy cargo across the river. Along the sides of the ramps leading from the river to the road above, as well as some areas along the road, wooden tubs waited their turn to receive the precious load.

Most of the vintners, including my father, belonged to the *Winzerverein,* or vintners association, a group of people who combined their resources to buy larger presses, maintain a guesthouse, and had cellars in the *Winzerhaus.*

Due to the hard times before, during, and after World War II, the vintners association had no money to update the old equipment, such as barrels made of durable but heavy oak. Also, my father still used my grandfather's, Karl Kilian's, *Legel* with his initials, KK, burned in on top.

One of these containers weighed approximately thirty to thirty-two pounds. Each bearer adjusted the straps affixed to the *Legel* to fit him.

Before the harvest, we had taken all wooden vats, tubs, and *Legels* out of their storage in damp cellars that prevented their drying out. To make them watertight, we filled them up with water for two days.

Being young and feeling invincible, I volunteered to be the carrier for my father. Living among the steep hills of my hometown had conditioned me for this kind of work.

After the harvest, I found work with the vintners association: pressing grapes. The huge amount of grapes necessitated an around-the-clock operation. The *Kelterhaus* was a two-storied building in which the grapes were pressed. The top floor contained the vats and presses. Unloading and weighing took place on the ground floor; below that were the upper and lower wine cellars, with their rows of empty barrels. A gravity pump transported the *Most,* or grape juice, into the waiting barrels.

I usually worked the *Kelter,* pressing grapes during the night, slept two or three hours in the morning and went "sparking"—an expression I had learned in America—until I went to *kelter* again in the evening. What energy.

A slack time developed after we loaded the presses with the crushed grapes, allowing the *Kelter* to squeeze the last drop out of the grapes. During this time the *Kellermeister,* or the man in charge of pressing and wine making, and I sat in a little room on the ground floor to catch our breath. He was a veteran from the Russian front, where he had served from the beginning to the end of the campaign in WWII. We were exchanging our experiences.

"Did I tell you about the time I almost blew up the *Gulaschkanone?"* he asked.

A Gulaschkanone is a unique contraption developed for the military to cook and bake for the soldiers in the field.

He continued, "I was a mess sergeant then and had a beautiful stew bubbling in the kettle and fresh bread and potatoes baking in the two ovens attached to the kettle. Ivan had broken through with one of his mass attacks. There were no troops between us and Ivan except some scattered units, which were hurriedly retreating towards us."

"Didn't you have any reserves to plug the gap?" I asked.

"There was only a small MP unit behind us, engaged in *Partisanenbekämpfung,* or fighting partisans. Those troops would not be arriving to help for some time. I did not want Ivan to have my stew and took a hand grenade, potato-masher type, unscrewed the top from the handle and took the delaying fuse out. Then I took three more tops of other hand grenades, attached them to the main grenade, which I hid under the Gulschkanone. I attached a wire to the charge and the lid of the kettle so that, if Ivan would break through and we had to leave, the Russians would open the lid of the kettle. But they would not eat my stew.

"Didn't you try to stop them before they would reach your kitchen?" I asked.

"I'll get to that in a moment, but first we have to change the presses."

I hoped he would tell me while we were loading the presses but he was keeping me in suspense until we were finished with the task. Settled down in the little room again he enjoyed my eagerness, slowly uncorked a bottle and poured us wine. We swirled the two-year-old Riesling in our glasses, sniffed the aroma, nodded approval and drank to each other. Then Jean took out a sandwich and slowly started to eat.

"Come on now!" I begged him to continue.

"Okay, let's see where I left off."

The guy was really enjoying my impatience.

"There were five of us in the company area. The CO had left to go to the front in the morning. So it was up to me as sergeant to set up defenses. Our kitchen was in a small stand of trees, well hidden from the air. In front was an open field over which Ivan would be coming. We would see him before he saw us. I deployed two men with rifles to the left and one to the right from me; I had a submachine gun and had the fifth man go with me out into the field behind a big boulder. We took with us a box of hand grenades. I told the kid, who was not too swift, 'You stay low, and all you have to do is unscrew the caps from the handle and then give me the grenade.'

"Figures started to appear over the distant rise, but they were too few to have been Russians. As they ran full speed toward us we realized they were the remnants of the German defenders. I stood up and waved to them to join us. We gained six men and a light machine gun. They were of great help to us. No sooner had we deployed them, and the Russians appeared. So, we couldn't do anything but wait.

"The Soviets must have guessed that the small wooded area before them would be defended, right?" I interrupted.

"Yes, they slowed down to regroup. We saw small figures running among them, most likely commissars trying to whip the troops into shape for the attack. Then they drew near in three skirmish lines, slowly approaching our positions." Sean took a sip of his wine before continuing.

"My position forward of our line of defense was very exposed, but since we did not have artillery support I thought I could use the available grenades and have the same effect as with a light mortar. I hoped that I could throw far enough to scatter some grenades among them to force them to the ground. The kid next to me was shaking with the sight of the Russians approaching us in great numbers. I told him to get down and stay there, hoping that he would calm down if he did not see them up close. I needed him to prepare the grenades for me."

"What a risk. How did he make it that far?" I asked.

"With a guardian angel and guidance from his comrades," Jean said; "On they came and I was getting scared myself with this flood running toward us. As they advanced closer to our range, our thin line, deployed along the edge of the woods, opened fire. Ivan knew now where the defenders' position was and I started to lope my *ersatz* mortars. Initially I did not reach them, but it slowed them down a bit."

Sean stopped and stared out the window into the night. He must have been reliving the situation. After a while he picked up his train of thought again.

"When they came in range, those exploding grenades had a devastating effect on them. Their troops had already suffered severe losses caused by the persistent firing coming from our defenses, especially the machine gun. You know, the MG42 could really rip them apart. Disheartened, they hit the ground. Then groups started to retreat. Our thin line mounted a counterattack: The Russians ran for their lives. When the MP unit finally arrived, Ivan had disappeared over the rise. At first, I could not get up; my knees were shaking so much. The kid had wet his pants but had kept unscrewing the potato mashers' handles.

"Going back to my beloved goulash cannon I noticed one of the MPs was trying to undo the lid of the kettle. I was too far away to warn him so I shot a burst over the guy's head with my machine pistol and he immediately hit the deck. He was mad. But when I later showed him the grenade under the contraption he became weak-kneed. I disarmed the hand grenade, and all the survivors had a hearty meal. Later my CO recommended me for the Iron Cross First Class.

"Now let's load the presses again for the last time this night," Sean finished.

We returning POWs went through a catharsis, gradually shedding the ghosts of the last six to nine years. Telling our experiences took the place of talking to a psychiatrist to help us deal with our memories. This process took time. Slowly our mental wounds healed. The recounting of anecdotes was vital and served as our treatment. Thus we poured one weight after another from us. The world disliked German soldiers and our new government did its utmost to appease the world. Consequently we confessed to each other to unburden ourselves.

I like compound nouns. They are explicit as well as picturesque. Most can express a sentiment or meaning in negative or positive ways.

The Nazis used compound nouns with great impact in propaganda slogans. One example is *Pflichtbewusstsein,* to be aware of one's duties. When politicians addressed citizens, the word duty implanted itself in their minds. Over the years, Pflichtbewusstsein evoked the appropriate and desired response, suppressing thoughts of rights. The expression *Bürgerpflicht,* citizen's obligation, slowly replaced the word *Bürgerrecht,* citizens' rights.

I was only twelve years old when a national contest required all college-preparatory students to write an essay under the slogan *Volksgemeinschaft—Schicksalsgemeinschaft,* Commonwealth of the People—Common Fate. A simpler saying would have been, *Mitgefangen-Mitgehangen,* caught together-hung together.

The propaganda machines were often prophetic in their wording, describing in macabre expressions things to come, especially in the songs of sacrifice and death.

Thus, after my and my comrades' return home in 1948, we had to absorb, analyze and digest all the changes the German population had begun making three years earlier.

The painstaking metamorphosis took place in stages.

For many years I have thought about the stories and tribulations of former comrades. Now, that I am equally exposed to stories told by my former enemies, our experiences become intertwined. Without taking sides, I have a warm feeling for each one of them, whether he is a German *Landser,* an American Dog Face or GI, a Grunt, a Tommy, or a French Poilu.

All of us endured similar experiences and hardships, or had come close to death or being maimed. We had seen close friends killed, or trying feverishly to dig a hole into frozen, sandy, muddy, or stony soil, or hiding behind a ridiculously small bush. Many of us survived exposure to freezing temperatures or scorching heat, days of being soaking wet, developing hypothermia with severe chills and shaking. We saw friend and foe being buried. A small cross or Star of David, or a down-turned rifle topped by a helmet, marks the last resting place of a fallen comrade.

Ruhe in Frieden, Rest in Peace.

TURNING POINT

Das geht so nicht weiter. Things cannot continue like this. In 1949 I came to the conclusion: I must not continue this life style. The exploits with Lor were not only adventurous but also exemplified a life a man longed for at my age. All the activities of a pirate, well, a civilized pirate. The money was there, and with it women and wine.

My parents and my sister were concerned. Finally, Ina took the initiative and waited for me to come home from my escapades late one night. Her most important statement, and the one that made the greatest impact on my thinking, was, "What if any of those girls become pregnant? You will be in dire straits with no means of support." My sister has always been my true friend and her frankness caused me to think. Still, the change from rebel to responsible citizen took time. But Ina had my attention.

I wrote to Tom Bunch, the sergeant of the MPs, whom I had met on the Liberty ship. As I was not allowed to write to him while I was a POW, almost four years had passed since we heard from each other. I contacted him at his home in North Carolina. In his answer he wondered why I had not written to him for three years. He could not believe that I came home only in 1948.

When he was stationed in *Regensburg,* Bavaria, in 1949, I saved some money to visit him: We had a lot of reminiscing to do. Because he worked for the Counter Intelligence Corps, he had opportunity to check me out. During my visit, Tom introduced me to his commanding officer, a colonel, who suggested that I apply for a visa to emigrate to the United States.

I promptly began the paperwork with the U.S. Consulate in Frankfurt, although Tom could not sponsor me while he was in the

Army. By law, sponsors had to live near the immigrant, so that he would not become a burden to the U.S. government. The start of the Korean Conflict resulted in another period of waiting because Tom had to stay in the service.

With the help and prodding of my sister, I enrolled at the *Private Dolmetscher Schule* in *Bad Kreuznach,* a Private Interpreters' College, to study English. After completion of the courses, I had to pass exams before a government board to become an official interpreter and translator. Most of my fellow students were considerably younger than I; all but one were girls.

Hans Klink, born in 1928, had been a prisoner at the infamous *Hungerlager,* or starving camp, run by the French near Bretzenheim, outside of Bad Kreuznach. Immediately after the war he was caught up in a sweep as a civilian. Although he spent only a few months in this camp, he suffered greatly in this horrible situation. Hans became my *Schicksalsbruder,* or brother-in-fate, among the gaggle of girls.

Only days into the semester, I realized that one friendly girl was not part of the giggling geckos. I buried myself in homework and also participated vigorously in the difficult class. Although my knowledge of spoken English was superior to that of my classmates, I did not have the slightest knowledge about grammar.

The problem with teaching and learning at this time was the lack of books. Many of the older books had been printed during the reign of the previous government and were, therefore, politically tainted. So we had to work from typed sheets of instructions. I studied faithfully, and the basics in grammar sank into my thick Teutonic skull.

ALMUT

Keep smiling.

The serious girl in our class had a dictionary with a list of over two hundred irregular verbs. Bad-mouthing members of the class are still insisting that I married her because of her dictionary. But she had other redeeming attributes: She was beautiful and did not take any guff from me. She tamed the pirate.

Almut attended the classes in order to improve her English and French. Being a gardening journeywoman, she wanted to study abroad. With the end of my piracy, her gardening stopped also. On the final exam I received a better grade in grammar than Almut did, because one of the professors did not like girls. After graduation, we were married on August 12, 1950.

My immigration papers were dormant; we added applications for Almut and later for Veit, our son. I looked for a job. Since I was living in the French Zone of Occupation, the demand for interpreters in English was minimal...until I heard of a training class for German civilians, conducted by the U.S. Air Force near its headquarters in Wiesbaden. With my credentials, I was welcomed.

First, I had to learn how to type on an American typewriter, which has a different letter placement than German ones. Grammar was again stressed. Two things I will always remember about this course: one is the tune to *The Grandfather's Clock* to which we had to learn the rhythm of typing; and the other, most adverbs end in – ly, a difficult rule for German speakers to remember.

At the end of the course in Wiesbaden, I found work at the intelligence branch of the U.S. Air Force. My main assignment was to interview German prisoners returning from the Soviet Union. We learned about many dark areas in the U.S.S.R. unknown to the West. Interesting was the fact that some industrial cities were not even on the map. I had to translate the interviews from German into English and submit them to the appropriate offices. When other assignments such as personal espionage were required—not conducive to the welfare of a married man—I looked for other employment.

A rift between America and France had developed and many U.S. troops stationed in France were evicted. They had to find other bases. The French were fighting their war in Indochina, later Vietnam, and needed to pull many occupying forces out of Germany.

The U.S. 2nd Armored Division was transferred from the area around Giessen, Hesse, to Bad Kreuznach, where they occupied prewar facilities of a German infantry division, including a hospital. Finally, I could apply as an official interpreter near our home. Because this was not a full-time position I had to work also as a medical secretary.

The installations for the American 57th Field Hospital had been totally renovated and covered almost double the space of the one I had known. In December 1943 I was a patient in this hospital while I was a Luftwaffenhelfer.

German actors had entertained the wounded and the sick. During one of their performances I met the famous Scandinavian actress Lale Anderson. She sang the German ballad *Lili Marlen,* which dates back to WWI. The song, based on the German taps melody, was later picked up by Marlene Dietrich and was popular with both sides of the conflict in WWII.

Tom Bunch was still in the service. Consequently, our immigration status was inactive. We had a child and needed an apartment. My father suggested and helped to build an apartment in his third floor attic. After a few months' labor, we moved into our precious abode: two and a half rooms, kitchen and bath. We had a perfect view above the roofs of the village to the north and south. In the east, we saw the Rhine rushing by.

Working for the 57th Field Hospital was an adventure. All German employees were included in the every-day life of the hospital. Colonel Whitaker was the CO of a staff of about fifteen doctors, surgeons and general practitioners, dentists and psychiatrists. In addition to my interpreting and translating assignments, I was attached to the general practitioners' station, which included the psychiatric ward. In addition, I had to fill in when the surgical secretary's workload was too heavy.

On one occasion I had to take her place at an emergency operation. I stood in the background, while the surgeon dictated the procedure. Then I had to rush out, transcribe my notes and collect the specimen to be shipped out for analysis. The general medical reports were standard and could be written without the doctor's input, except for the corrections before the final signing.

To substitute for the hospital secretary was a job I dreaded. The Morning Report was a nightmare for me. By requirement, I had to type the report in quadruplicate without any corrections. I, literally, typed it one letter at a time, scared of having to start over again if I made a typo.

As interpreter and translator I had to certify documents that involved the German government of the city of Bad Kreuznach, such as birth certificates and marriage licenses.

Because every newborn in Germany is of German nationality at birth, I verified the information on the German certificate of babies born at the 57th Field Hospital, so that the U.S. authorities in Frankfurt could change the child's status to U.S. citizen.

One day I had to rush to the local registrar's office after several dictations pertaining to circumcisions. At the marriage ceremony between one of our doctors and his German bride, the registrar mentioned *Umstände,* or circumstances, in his speech. My translation came out as circumcisions. Shocked I looked at the groom who was one of our surgeons. He winked at me and saved the day. From then on I performed my patterned wedding ceremony translation, regardless of what the registrar said.

Years later, when I was a member of the Stuart Corinthian Yacht Club, I met a man who had been hospitalized at the 57th during my employment there. I must have typed his medical report. Small World.

The first doctor attending patients on the Psychiatric Ward was M. Bernard Hecht from New York City, the most laid-back person I ever met. On the day he asked me if I had time for an extended lunch, we went downtown to his apartment where lunch consisted of saltine crackers and peanut butter. That describes Dr. Hecht. We had a long talk, which I suspect was a session for him to get into the mind of a German who had lived the bad times. I did not mind his motives. We were friends while he was stationed at the 57th.

His successor was Dr. Merle R. Ingraham. Merle was always on the go, searching for new experiences, becoming involved in the German culture. Merle's wife, Margaret, eventually joined him in Germany. She had to live off the compound because Merle's assignment was for eleven months. Dependents received military lodging only if the soldier was abroad for one year or longer.

Margaret was pregnant during their stay in Germany. She gave birth to a girl, Jaimye Sue, in Bad Kreuznach, the same town where our Veit was born a year earlier. Thus began a life-long friendship between our two families.

Dr. Ingraham knew that we were trying to emigrate to the United States. He offered to sponsor us if Tom Bunch who was still in the service could not do so. On Merle's return to Greenfield, Massachusetts, we filed applications again and soon the bureaucracy began to churn. Not long afterward we received our visas.

During the time our papers were processed, the U.S. Consulate sent me a peculiar letter, questioning me as to why I had not reported that I had been a member of the Nazi party. This was news to me. Upon reflection I realized that the Nazis automatically entered former members of the Hitler Youth into the party on their eighteenth birthday. I wrote to the consulate and explained that on the very day I was transferred to the party I had become a prisoner of war. I could not have had anything to do with the transfer. I even gave them my POW number, 81G401060, and asked them to check my records with the war department. The consulate accepted my explanation.

Our days were hectic now. Almut and I had to dissolve our way of life, getting rid of most of our possessions; selling whatever we could to pay for our tickets on the ocean liner *Gripsholm.* Almut was pregnant again and we could not take a plane because of her advanced state. So *Gripsholm* it was.

The *Gripsholm* had been a Swedish Red Cross ship during the war. In 1954 the German line *Norddeutscher Loyd* acquired her. We joined this ocean liner on the voyage to New York. When she left New York again, she became known as the *Berlin;* years later she was dismantled.

Our relatives found it hard to see us go into an unknown future. The turmoil of the preparations left little time to contemplate our move. We strongly believed in our determination and ability to build a more promising life in the New World. Almut's parents drove us to Hamburg from where we took a train to Bremerhaven, the German port of debarkation for ships sailing to the United States. The passage was to take ten days.

After we came on board, a steward guided us to our cabin. While stowing our luggage we heard a knock on the cabin door.

"Surprise! I wanted to wish you a safe crossing and good luck in America," said Herbert May.

"How did you find us?" I asked my good friend and fellow POW in Scotland, the former submariner.

"I called your parents," he said.

After Herbert left the POW camp in Scotland he obtained his captain's license and now commanded a small tanker on rivers and in the costal trade. His vessel was tied up in Bremerhaven. So he took the time to say goodbye to us.

In recent years, Herbert had visited us several times when he came up the Rhine. We in turn went with him down the river from Bingen to Trechtingshausen on our first visit to Germany in 1966. His son spent vacations on board with his parents but lived with grandparents during the school year. The boy's pet was a rabbit whose favorite place was under the heavy cast-iron rudder segment on the stern. He loved chocolate and thumped his feet when a stranger came aboard.

On board the ocean liner, we exchanged memories with Herbert before saying, hopefully, "Auf Wiedersehen," or till we meet again.

The *Gripsholm* left Bremerhaven late in the day on 23 November 1954.. We stood on deck to watch the band play *"Muss I denn, muss I denn zum Städtele hinaus...?"* Do I have to leave this town? And we wanted to wave farewell to Herbert, who looked like only a pin's head in the throng of relatives and friends on the pier. We said goodbye also to the land of our births, ready to face our challenges in America.

Shortly after the ship put out to sea we went to dinner. Our assignment was to eat at the first settings and to have our own table, an advantage because we could help three-year-old Veit when he had difficulty managing his food during rough seas.

The passage through the channel was smooth. Dover was clearly visible. It appeared strange to me to see it "from the other side." I recognized the navy prison, which had been my home for a while.

The first two days out of Bremerhaven were calm but then at night, off the coast of Ireland, a hurricane hit us. Most of the passengers, and even a third of the crew, were seasick.

The food on board was great but due to heavy seas we did not consume much. The dining room crew wetted down the tablecloths to prevent the dishes from sliding off the table. Breakfast was served in one sitting and in the afternoon, so were coffee and cake in the German tradition. We ate supper at six o'clock, and sandwiches were available at ten.

Our table steward did everything in his power to help our little boy who suffered next to seasickness also a cold, headaches and earaches. Veit was a good trooper and spent most of his time in the ship's *Kindergarten*.

Another storm hit us off Halifax, Nova Scotia. Passengers had to spend most of the time below deck. So that the personnel could move about, the crew installed life lines on deck. We rented some deckchairs in the glassed-in section of the vessel. Wrapped in blankets, we could at least get some fresh air. Our steward praised the *Gripsholm* for her seaworthy construction. "Modern ships are built for speed and are more susceptible of heavy sea movement."

Our trusted vessel had to make a landfall in Halifax for about two hours. An elderly Canadian had died of a heart attack due to the severe weather conditions. His son came to Halifax to pick up the body.

For good measure, a third storm whipped up the seas on our last leg of this voyage, our passage to New York.

"I'll never go on a ship again," Veit declared.

Entering the harbor of New York, we met a freighter coming out, greeting us with horn blowing and dipping of the flag. Another German vessel. With odd feelings we saw her disappear in the direction of Germany. Passing the statue of Liberty, we focused our thoughts on the future.

The *Gripsholm* tied up at 1:00 PM on 4 December 1954. Soon we stood waiting in long lines to pass immigration, inching along for almost three hours. I had to carry Veit on my arm most of the time. The delay was not the fault of the American officials but due to the fact that we were one of the first groups of immigrants not to go through Ellis Island. After a short checking of the papers, we received a friendly "Welcome to America" by the official. He handed us our landing passes, and shortly afterwards we set foot on American soil.

The next task was to look for our luggage among the hundreds of bags and crates lined up on the dock. I discovered one Metzroth suitcase. Almut and Veit stayed with it while I searched for the rest.

Some of the containers came badly damaged out of the holds of the vessel. After I found all our suitcases and trunks, I located a shipping company to send the heaviest containers directly to Greenfield. The rest I loaded on a luggage carrier, and we headed towards the exit.

Merle, our sponsor, was already waiting for us behind the exit barrier.

"Hey, it's good to see your friendly face in all this commotion." I said. "Where is Margaret?"

"You'll meet her at the hotel where we'll all stay for the night."

114

In the evening we did some sightseeing and went to eat at an automat, picking our meals from little "coffins."

"So many new experiences already on the first day in America," Almut said.

Veit quietly observed the street scenes, pointing at cars, window displays, and people. "I can't understand anyone but you," he said to us in German.

"You will," I assured him. "Mutti and I had to learn it, too."

After paying our hotel bill—$13.00—the next morning we left for our trip north. Driving along the Hudson River brought back memories of my return trip down the river as a POW six years earlier. And I thought I might never see New York again.

Soon we were on our way through Connecticut. Five hours later we reached Greenfield, Massachusetts, our future home for more than thirty-three years until 1989 when we moved to Florida.

Our first transportation in Greenfield.

LIVING IN GREENFIELD, MASSACHUSETTS

So, this is Merle's hometown.

Nestled between the Connecticut River and the foot of the Berkshires, Greenfield typified a small New England town. Early settlers cultivated the land and established prosperous farming communities. Later, industries took advantage of the Connecticut and Green rivers to power their factories; and of the east-west as well as north-south crossroads on which to transport their goods.

In 1954 the Greenfield Tap and Die Company was the leading manufacturer in America producing metal-cutting tools. At the Millers Falls Tool Company skilled craftsmen manufactured hand tools and eventually developed power tools.

Lunt Silversmiths, another well-known employer in Greenfield, is the only one of the named three local manufacturers still producing in that town. Many American brides have selected their place settings from Lunt's silverware patterns.

Channing L. Bete added to Greenfield's reputation with his Scriptography, a series of informational booklets in which cartoon-like figures explain a wide variety of subjects from grammar to medical topics.

For the first weeks after our arrival in Greenfield we stayed with the Ingrahams in their house on Cooke Street. Their entire family, including Grandpa and Grandma Ingraham and all the Newcombs from Merle's maternal side, invited us for Christmas and had some wonderful gifts. They adopted our little son as grandparents do and included us in their family. The Newcombs belonged to a long line of New England farmers; to be exposed to their traditional lifestyle was enlightening. Charley and Mable Newcomb with Maverette, their only daughter, were a warmhearted family who always had the welcome-door open.

In January I hoped to make some money shoveling snow. Our resources were running low and we did not want to be too much of a burden to Merle and Margaret.

By the end of December, I landed a job as produce man in a neighborhood supermarket. What a relief! I could bring home $35.00 a week and could start to look for an apartment.

Almut was getting to the end of her pregnancy. Our little son Nicord was born on 20 January 1955. Merle had taken Almut to the hospital in the morning; I had to go to work because we needed the money.

In the afternoon I was wrapping some produce in the back when Merle came to see me. I was delighted when he told me that Almut had delivered a boy, but then he sadly added that our son only lived for a few hours because he was born with an open spine.

I took time off and went to the hospital to see Almut. She was heartbroken that she could not even hold our little boy in her arms. A kind nurse said that she could arrange for me to see Nicord. She put the little one into my arms, I opened the blanket and saw the most beautiful tiny face, lips parted, appearing to be asleep. I did not want to hand him back to the nurse, but eventually I covered his face again and said goodbye to our little son.

The next day we buried Nicord. We were poor and did not have any money to buy a plot, so he was laid to rest in the paupers' section of the cemetery. After a year, we could give him a headstone. Little did we know when we came to the States, that so soon we would take possession of a small plot of American ground. It was a sad beginning for us but the stark circumstances gave us little time to grieve. We treasured our growing son, Veit, all the more.

In the spring we moved into our first apartment on Pond Street.

"Oh, Bert! I was so impressed with the fact that we'd be the first tenants of these newly created living quarters that I didn't consider this former attic might be insufficiently insulated. It's just unbearably hot during the day."

"*Ja, Vati.* We have to go shopping to grand Union every day because the butter melts and the milk tastes icky."

"Icky, huh? Where did you learn that word?" I asked.

"Greg said it when he held a worm yesterday."

We found another apartment two houses down the street. What a difference the brick building made in the summer heat. The neighborhood was full of children. It did not take long for Veit to learn his friends' language. We continued to speak German at home so he would be bilingual.

On 5.5.55 I started a job with Minott Printing and Binding as a proofreader and was now bringing home the astronomical sum of $50.00 a week. The company was printing mainly catalogs and price sheets for the local industries. Minott's was an all-letterpress organization. At the time, offset was being introduced and many printers were changing to offset presses. I am glad though to have been exposed to the methods of typesetting with Mergenthaler hot-metal casters and hand composition.

Most of my proofreading entailed reading price sheets, a boring task. I gradually involved myself with preparations of artwork for letterpress plates and took an art course to expand my capabilities. My work shifted from proofreading to art preparation and layouts. In order to stay competitive, the company acquired offset presses, and with this change I was placed in charge of the prep department. After the procurement of a 12foot bed 20x24 camera, stripping tables and contact frames, Minott's became independent and did not have to deal with outside prep houses. I enjoyed my work immensely and soon became proficient in the field. In addition, I did some consulting work in layout and artwork for other printing companies.

With the progression in my job, wages increased accordingly and we soon could afford a visitor from Germany, my father. In the cellar of the house on Pond Street was a small workroom where my father built us some badly needed furniture, such as dressers and bookcases. We had recently finished buying our beds on the installment plan. A man came by every week and collected seventy-five cents for our mattresses. We adjusted quickly to the American way of installment payments; we had to, otherwise we would not have had beds for some time.

It is incredibly difficult for a foreigner to adept to the American way of life. There is also a lot of hidden fear, *will we make it?* In retrospect, I would not want to do it again. Our youth helped us to overcome all obstacles. With Almut's resourcefulness we bought a *bicycle* which I used to go to work. The bike was also handy when we walked it to the swimming pool in the summer; it carried all our gear and Veit. A three-mile hike at that time did not faze us, but eventually we had to take the big step and look for a car. The dealer introduced us to another American way of doing things: borrowing money. He went with me to the bank, and with a $300 loan, we became the proud owners of a 1949 Nash.

Our car resembled an overturned bathtub and was very roomy, a *playpen of sorts* for Veit. Of course, the Nash had standard shift. The *innovation* on this car was a lever under the dashboard that allowed us to engage the overdrive. We bought the car when it registered ninety thousand miles on the odometer. After two years, and after the odometer had turned over to zero and began counting the miles anew, we had to trade our treasure in because the front-wheel bearing gave out. The next car was a *much smaller* '54 Chevy. Veit had to adjust.

But before that, our son Riko was born in December 1955.

Veit was elated to, finally, being a big brother.

Gradually we melted into the general population and began to think about purchasing a home of our own. We needed more space when Eitel, born in October 1959, joined our growing family. With the help of Almut's parents we could afford a down payment on a house on Graves Road in the northern part of Greenfield.

Think for Yourself

Veit missed his grandparents and cousins. Every year at Thanksgiving he told us that his friends went to eat dinner at their grandma's table.

"Can't Oma and Opa come to visit us? We have enough room for them, don't we?" he asked.

My parents were delighted to come from Germany to see their American grandchildren. "How can we help?" they asked in word and deed. Oma's cooking and sewing relieved Almut and spoiled our sons. Opa's carpentry skills produced toys for our boys; but more than that, they fulfilled a wish for our family.

"I need a boat, Papa. Do you think we could build one from a kit?" I asked.

"Where do you want to build it? You can't just do that in your backyard without protection from the weather."

"I have a place in mind. First, let's order this kit," I said as I showed Papa a Luger catalog. "What do you think of this twenty-one-foot cabin cruiser?"

"Well, we could start it together..."

The next day I approached my employer, "Mr. Minott, I plan to build a boat. Would you allow me to use the plant's empty backroom for my project?"

"A boat? How would you get it out of there when finished?"

"I have a trailer. First, we will build the hull upside down on the ground. When the hull is assembled we will turn it over. Then we place it on the trailer with the help of the printing crew."

"This endeavor I have to see. Go ahead. You may use the electricity."

We were in business. Or were we? For days my father and I tried to follow the kit's instructions but could not fit certain parts together.

I called the Luger company, "Are you sure you sent me the correct plans?" After I quoted the model number on the instructions, the company representative said slowly, "No-o, we will send you the appropriate papers."

My confidence in my ability to read directions was restored.

By the time my parents had to return to Germany, the work on the vessel was far enough advanced that I could trailer it home. I finished the construction in our yard.

"What name shall we give our boat?" I asked my family one evening at the dinner table. Within minutes, twelve-year-old Veit had the answer.

"Let's call her BRAVE."

"Brave?"

"Yes, for *Bert, Riko, Almut, Veit, Eitel,*" Veit said triumphantly.

And so we launched our BRAVE on a lake in Massachusetts, hoping that she would float. She did, and for a few years we enjoyed family excursions on the Connecticut River. Our most ambitious outing was a voyage on Lake Champlain, going north into Canada on the Richelieu River.

ALMUT BECOMES A TEACHER

In 1961 a new epoch in our life began when a teacher of German at the local high school approached Almut to take over his position since he was going to teach in Japan at an American school.

Almut agreed and obtained a state waiver for teaching. Next, we had to secure the help of a babysitter to take care of our two-year-old Eitel. A friend's mother was delighted to take this job. Eitel was a happy and cooperative child and Mrs. Schneider was the right grandmotherly caretaker for him. For the first two years of teaching, Almut made so little money that we broke even after the expenses for the babysitter. We had to consider the future benefits if Almut were to continue to teach. An additional burden for her was the requirement to attend classes at the University of Massachusetts in order to study the educational block and earn eighteen credits from the School of Education.

We were sorry but Mrs. Schneider was getting too old to be a safe babysitter for Eitel, so we decided to enroll our son at the Roberts School in Shelburne. Eitel, the always-cheerful boy, adapted to the situation exceedingly well.

Now we needed a second car for one of us to take him to the Roberts School bus stop. A used Packard was the answer to our problem. We could buy this old luxury car at a reasonable price; reasonable, we discovered, because of a questionable transmission. Nevertheless, after repairs the car served its purpose.

Almut managed her three-fold job of taking care of our family, teaching school and taking classes at the university. Many a time I wondered whether it was worth all the trouble she went through, but she was a trouper and kept going. I helped her as much as I could, but I knew that it was never enough to relieve her of the burdens she shouldered.

With time, our lot improved to the point where Almut's income had progressed from the red to the black and we could think of relocating from the outskirts to the vicinity of schools and Minott's. The summer of this move was a complete upheaval for us.

We sold our house on Graves Road and had to vacate it before the construction of our new domicile on Green Street was finished. Where were we going to stay during the summer? A good friend and fellow teacher at the high school learned that a neighbor and his family were spending several weeks in Colorado and needed a house sitter. Perfect. We moved the furniture into the two-car garage of our temporary summer place and lived in South Deerfield until September.

Our new house in Greenfield had hardwood floors throughout that had to be finished with several coats of polyurethane. After work I sanded and painted ad nauseum until it was dark. Although the windows were wide open, I think I was high after a few hours of this activity.

At the same time, Almut commuted to the university to study during the summer sessions. Since Private Interpreters' College in Germany was not a liberal arts college, she was now laboring for her Bachelor's degree. My woman had stamina. Our boys were cooperative throughout this whole ordeal and helped as much as they could with the household chores.

Also in 1961 Almut, Veit and I joined Riko and Eitel as U.S. citizens and sponsored Almut's parents. The following year they immigrated to our chosen country and lived with us in Greenfield until they became acclimated and independent. I was able to arrange for my father-in-law to work in my department at Minott Printing, a job he kept until his retirement at age sixty-five.

In our new house we finally settled down to an orderly pace as much as possible. Again our sons were of great help painting walls and cleaning up the mess we made in the process. Almut was now in charge of the Foreign Language Department at Greenfield High

School. With our combined income we could think of a luxury item that had been on our mind for a long time, a sailboat.

Cruising the Bahamas

FINALLY SAILING

Since the years I lived near the Rhine, mostly *on* the Rhine as a boy, I have been obsessed by the desire to feel the movement of something afloat under my feet. After chartering a thirty-foot Bristol in Camden, Maine, we were hooked, that is, I was hooked, but my family liked sailing too, despite a rough ending of our charter period.

We had explored Penobscot Bay for a whole week. On the last night, we anchored at Butter Island on the eastern part of the bay. After a beautiful day of exploring the island, we settled down for the night. The sea was calm and the sky serene. The air felt peaceful, almost eerily peaceful. In the morning we woke up to pea-soup fog and could barely see the bow pulpit from the cockpit.

"What now, Dad?" Veit asked. "Aren't we supposed to return the boat to the yard today?"

"Maybe we can stay here until the fog lifts," Riko said.

"No, no! This is Sunday. I have to go to work tomorrow. Let's look at the chart and determine our course back to Camden."

"Are you sure the compass has been corrected?" Almut asked.

"We have the local variation on the chart. I hope that the charter company compensated for the deviation in the compass. I should have checked that before leaving Camden," I answered.

Lobster pots dot the sea near a chain of islands and the outlying ledges from Butter Island to Camden. So that I would not miss the island we were headed for, I had to take a course toward the middle of it; in case the compass was off somewhat, I still would not miss the island. Once I approached it, I had to turn to port and run along the edge of the lobster ledge using the depth sounder to determine the ledge. I hoped to pick up a shadow of the dark trees on the island.

"All right. Veit, you sit at the pulpit and sing out every lobster pot you spot. As soon as you see one, indicate with your arms where a marker is floating. Almut, stand at the main and relay Veit's directions to me. Riko, station yourself amidships on port, Eitel on starboard, to be sure to give each float a wide berth. We don't want a prop wrap."

The boys were excited to be assigned their respective watches, despite Riko's initial doubts about leaving in the fog.

After pulling the anchor we motored cautiously west. Lightning flashed through the fog. We heard thunderclaps.

"The storm is out at sea. According to weather reports we should be safe, or we would have stayed at anchor," I said to my crew.

When the rain started, visibility was cut down even more.

We poked our way by compass towards the island. Hours later we made landfall. Fortunately the fog cleared somewhat and we could see the contour of the island. Labyrinthing through the minefield of pots, we finally reached the outer buoy of Camden's harbor; the fog lifted and we could enter our destination.

With the charter voyage successfully completed, we decided to buy a sailboat and make Camden our home harbor. The dealer in Marblehead, Massachusetts, had an Ericson 27 and an Ericson 29 on display. After some soul-searching we decided on the larger model to have enough room for our growing boys. The boat was equipped with an inboard Atomic 4 gas engine. We took delivery late that season and had to sail the boat to Camden on a long weekend because our vacations were over.

The passage was enjoyable except for a little incident which later turned into an expensive consequence. The discharge hose of the head came with a weak spot that, after some use, developed a leak allowing a slow seepage of seawater into the bilge. Slowly the saltwater accumulated in the bilge to a level that submerged part of the flywheel and, when the engine was running, sprayed a light salty mist into the carburetor air intake. This deposit did not impair the performance of the engine immediately but when the boat was laid up for the winter, the salt deposit caused the engine to lock up and refuse to start in the spring. The repair cost, which the boat builder had to pay, was extensive.

Frustrated because the engine never performed reliably after the repair, we decided to re-power our BRAVE II with a Universal diesel.

Now a happily purring engine backed up our sails. We cruised Penobscot Bay during the summer vacations and weekends for five years, avoiding lobster pots and honing our sailing skills.

The summers in Maine are short, especially as far east as Camden. When the United States experienced a fuel shortage in 1974, we had to reduce the mileage of our trips from Greenfield to the boat and chose Kennebunkport, Maine, for our new homeport. At that time K'port, as we called it, was a quiet but growing maritime town with an artists' colony. Summer tourism has a long tradition there as the big established hotels prove.

Later on, when President George H.W. Bush used his summer domicile on Walker's Point, the tourists flocked to K'port. We always knew when the President was in town because a large Coast Guard cutter anchored off the harbor entrance. We saw Mr. Bush many times as we came into the harbor or as he went out with his speed boat, always friendly with a nod or an "Isn't it a glorious day?" One day we observed the President hanging over the transom to free the propeller from a lobster pot line and a secret service man holding on to Mr. Bush's pants to prevent him from falling overboard.

Our family sailing days in Maine were unforgettably beautiful. Eventually though, as our sons grew up, they could not accompany us regularly because of school activities and because Veit entered Williams College in Williamstown, Massachusetts.

All three of our boys chose to take German in school with their mother as the teacher. In 1972 Almut began to offer to her students bi-annual educational tours to Europe during spring break. I accompanied the groups as a male chaperon.

For a number of years we chose Iceland Air to Luxembourg. What was so amazing about the first year was the price of only $189.00 for flight, transportation and hotels in Germany. Landing in Luxembourg was of great advantage to us because its airport had a rural setting. Thus we did not have to deal with large airport traffic.

During the war in Vietnam, Veit's draft number was forty. He married before he was scheduled to leave for Asia. To his great fortune, hostilities ended two months before he graduated from college.

METZROTH GRAPHICS

I had my own war to fight in the early seventies as far as my job was concerned. Greenfield experienced plant closings or relocations of their two main employers and taxpayers, the Millers Falls Tool Company and the Greenfield Tap and Die factories. Due to these developments Minott Printing had difficulty staying afloat. All of the staff and workers tried valiantly to keep the plant going.

The stress and uncertainty caused me to break down. I could not go to work. Almut called Dr. Ingraham who had me on my feet in a day. This occurrence forced me to make a decision. *Look for another job or start your own business.* I chose the latter and established Metzroth Graphics. Almut's income sustained us for the first twelve months.

Over the years I had developed a list of clients with whom I could deal after Minott Printing closed their business. A local advertising firm, The Agency, was interested in in-house preparations and suggested I rent space from them. This solution benefited both firms.

The need for more graphic equipment and room to place it soon became obvious. My first camera proved to be too small and had to be replaced by a larger one, a twelve-foot process camera. *It will never fit in here; neither will the necessary light tables and contact frame.*

"How do you feel about moving to larger premises?" I asked Bruce Woodard, the co-owner of The Agency.

"Can you keep up with the growth of your business?"

"There will not be any growth without improved space for my equipment," I answered.

"Okay, let's find a suitable place."

131

We moved our businesses into larger quarters in back of offices, where I built my studio, darkroom and camera room. By that time Metzroth Graphics was relatively well established and separate from the ad agency. On occasion, I had to hire temporary help to keep up with the demand.

I gained recognition for creating artwork as well as plate-ready negatives and positives for the trade and developed a technique with mezzotints that my competitors did not offer. For the University of Massachusetts I used this technique in designing brochures of quality superior to simple halftone reproductions, setting them apart from average brochures.

Pneumo Precision of Keene, New Hampshire, was my largest client. The founder of the company had formerly worked as an engineer for Miniature Ball Bearings, a leader in its field. At Pneumo Precision, Don, the owner, developed pneumatic bearings where spindles ran on air. This action required such high tolerances that the company had to build its own measuring equipment for laces and routers.

"What are the bearings' measurements?" I asked the inventor.

"When you split a hair into one thousand parts, that's the unit we measure with."

Pneumatic bearings were a new field for the advertising department of the company, too. They could not find any copywriters to explain the capacity of the machines. Once, after I employed a copywriter, an engineer read the text and looked at me. He grinned.

"What kind of gobbledygook is this? I'll have to write it myself."

A thousand dollars down the drain of Metzroth Graphics. "Please write your own copy from now on," I said. Asking an engineer to write his own copy was a delicate maneuver.

My rapport with the ad department was excellent. The employees appreciated it when I tried to talk them out of expensive ideas without charging them for advice.

Designing brochures for Pneumo Precision was interesting and challenging because it opened a completely new field of endeavor. The tolerances in measurements were so critical that only a computer could guide the machines. When the equipment was metal-cutting fine surfaces, suction tubes were installed so that the flakes would not touch the surface of the work piece and mar it. The machines were mounted on four-by-eight-by-four-feet granite blocks, which in turn sat on air bags to muffle any vibrations coming from a truck driving several hundred feet away.

Don went to lunch with me one day. Before we left, he started to slowly spin the shaft in the pneumatic bearing. Two hours and some Martinis later we came back: The spindle was still spinning.

I had designed a four-page color brochure for Pneumo Precision for a show in Chicago. Since the printer did not deliver in time, I had to fly the pamphlets out to the exhibit. Our son, Riko, was living in Hoffmans Estate at the time and working in Chicago. I used the opportunity to take Almut with me to make the delivery and also visit with Riko and his wife, Gretchen.

The show was an eye-opener for me. Sue, the woman in charge of advertising for Pneumo Precision, drew my attention to a group of Japanese visitors at the show.

"Keep an eye on them and observe how they operate. Over the years we learned their mode of operation and tried to neutralize them."

"What do you mean by *neutralize them?*"

"The men come in groups. Every one in the group has his own assignment that appears rather harmless. We learned fast and did our best not to deal with them."

"But they would buy your equipment if you dealt with them," I said.

"Bert, you're as naïve as we used to be. They are not here to buy, they are to spy and steal our ideas. Now watch them closely and observe their techniques."

Soon the first Japanese of his group ambled up to our stand and wanted to know whether we had a brochure for him. Sue had pushed the stack of printing material under the table and told him we were out of sales brochures. While we were talking to the first Japanese man, another one came by and tried to measure the size of the machine. Now Sue told him politely to desist. In the meantime the third tried to take a picture of another spy in front of the machine. Sue rushed to the photographer and stood in front of him to prevent him from taking his picture. I saw a fourth man measuring the dimensions of the granite block. I casually moved over and bumped him so he lost his tape measure inside the machine. Then I excused myself profusely. When I looked up, Sue grinned at me.

"You're learning. Now you know what we're up against."

Sue and the two engineers had their hands full, fending the different groups off and still trying to make some sales to others.

When we later met in Keene after the show she told me that we received first prize for the printed brochure; another feather in my cap.

While I built up my business, our family grew up as well. Riko, our pre-med major, graduated from Skidmore College, but in order to make some money before continuing his studies, he worked for an insurance company.

Our first grandson, Veit's son, was born. Erik was a delight to have around. He spent many a week with his grandparents, especially on the boat in Maine.

Five-year-old Erik did not want to use the word bathroom in public. One day we were driving on Route 1 by Ogunquit, Maine. Our grandson, who could read, said, "Let's say Ogunquit instead of bathroom, okay?" We have been using the name since.

On Sundays we usually left K'Port late in the evening to drive home. One beautiful moonlit night Erik was lying in the back of the station wagon and was admiring the moon.

"Did you know, Erik, I can move the moon from one side of the car to the other?" I asked.

"No, you can't," he replied.

"Yes, I can. I only have to collect some force in me and when I have it I'll show you."

When a curve came up, I called to him, "I have enough power now and I am moving the moon from the right side to the left."

Sure enough the moon moved from the right to the left side. Our grandson was speechless for a while, contemplating the power his wondrous grandfather possessed.

"Do it again for me now," he called out after a while.

We were on a straight road. What to do?

"I cannot do it immediately, because I have to collect my force again, I depleted it with the first try. I'll let you know when I have refurbished my power."

Soon a new curve came in sight and I told him that I almost had enough power to move the moon again.

That's why there is a grand in front of grandparents.

Meanwhile, Erik completed his Master's degree at Old Dominion University.

Our youngest son, Eitel, came home one afternoon during his senior year at high school and said, "I enlisted in the Marine Corps." Bam, just like that. What could we say? We just hoped that he would not have to serve during a war.

"I can take it. It cannot be worse than the work-out we got from our coaches of the football team."

He went with our blessings. Today he still walks like a Marine.

For Eitel's graduation from boot camp at Parris Island, South Carolina, Almut and I flew to Jacksonville, Florida, and rented a car to attend his graduation. Before driving to Parris Island, we took an excursion west in the direction of Camp Blanding near Starke, Florida, where I had been a POW. I was eager to see what had happened to the camp after 1946.

As we approached the area we came to a large gate with the name "Camp Blanding." Inside the gate I noticed some WWII warehouses with the loading platforms in front. I had never seen these before because we prisoners never came this far out.

"There is a lake to your right, did you know that?" Almut said.

"No, but I had heard about it. It's Kingsley Lake. Our prisoner band used to play for the Saturday dances at the NCO club."

On we went haphazardly. I did not know my way because I had seen the area only from the back of a truck to and from work. Soon we neared a small building with the sign "Camp Commander." I left Almut in the car, not knowing what to expect. A friendly officer greeted me and was very interested in my past and connection to the camp. We were lost in conversation and checking maps of the camp when Almut, tired of waiting in the Florida heat and humidity, entered the building.

After a while the officer invited us to follow him in our car as he showed us around. When we stepped out of the administrative building I realized that the hangar about three hundred yards from us was the former tailor and shoe repair shop of my time, but the officer did not let us go close or enter it.

Following the officer we soon came to the refrigeration building. The same unit where I had arrived by train in 1944. Opposite the building were the remnants of the forty warehouses in one of which I worked as an interpreter. Only the poured concrete blocks, on which the warehouses once stood, were left. The warehouses were gone.

Now I knew where I was. When the officer left us, I reconnoitered further and found the road that led the way to our camp. We had to travel over a small bridge and up a hill. At the top we came to the former entrance that led into the POW compound. The officer had warned us that there was a rifle range for the National Guard, so we did not go any farther than the entrance. The whole area was covered with trees that had grown for forty years since I left. We barely could make out the road and the drainage ditch. On the way out of the camp we also discovered the chimney of the boiler for the laundry. I took a piece of a rotten 2x4 with me as a reminder of the finality in the course of life.

THE BIRTH OF
TRANSGRAPHICS

During our summers in Maine we became acquainted with a fellow sailor in the Arundel Boatyard, the marina where we docked our boat. Gordon Oburg was a retired army officer who had served in the 82nd Airborne in WWII. While talking about our respective military service during the war, I mentioned that I was in the German 4th Airborne Division. From then on he was always asking about my experiences. Gordon was gung-ho about his time of active duty and complained frequently that I did not talk about mine.

Being an old "Maineiac", Gordon had many relatives in K'port and knew the area well. He introduced us to many points of interest.

Gordon owned a Cape Dory 27. As a single sailor, he was always under way to explore the nearby islands. Because he was retired, he could afford the time. Meticulous about his charts, he maintained them diligently according to the corrections published by the bi-weekly *Notice to Mariners.*

One day I walked over to Gordon who worked on his boat. I was about to turn back because of his continued grumbling, when he saw me. He looked up helplessly and said, "Bert, you're an artist. How would you handle these corrections without messing up the chart?"

His fingers were stained with India ink, so was the tip of his nose. Kneeling in the cockpit in front of his locker, he represented such a miserable picture, I wanted to laugh. Gordon being such a curmudgeon in the truest sense of the word, I swallowed my amusement and gave him some hints. "Most of all, work on a decent surface instead of the cockpit locker. The India ink will seep under your templates of the various shapes of buoys. Use a dark pencil and keep it sharp. You can use the India ink to write the numbers, but not for the templates," I said.

"How do the mariners on ships keep up with corrections? They have stacks of charts to update every two weeks, or every time they leave port," he moaned.

"That I can tell you. I heard about it from a fellow artist in Greenfield. Ray was stationed in Norfolk during WWII in the headquarters of a submarine fleet. All during the war, he did nothing but correct charts for the navy. Ray said they finally gave up using templates and pictured them in free hand. That's what you should do, too."

"Free hand," he screamed, "I'm not a damn artist like you!"

"Gordon, I'm just giving you the advice you asked for."

"I don't need some damn Kraut to make fun of me!"

"Come on, Gordon, let me know where the corrections are and I will free-hand them in for you."

He calmed down and was soon on his favorite topic, WWII.

"If we had been against your elite division we would have licked you in no time," he said.

"Gordon, if we had fought against each other, with equal supplies and air support, in all likelihood neither one of us would be alive now."

"You were that good?" he grinned.

"Adequate." I grinned back.

"Then why don't you tell me about it some time?"

"The war is over, Gordon, be glad of it."

On the way home from K'port, I had ample time to think about our conversation. There really should be a better way to handle these continuous changes of the charts.

By the time we got home, I had a glimmer of an idea but was too tired to continue focusing on it. The next morning, though, the idea was growing in my head to the extent that I could not concentrate on other business.

Okay, you can do it! It's a matter of combining your graphic arts background with your knowledge of seamanship. After all, you only have to transfer some images on paper. That's what you have been doing for the last thirty-five years.

I've got it! TRANSFER!

For years I had been working with Chartpack, preparing positive films for the silk-screening company in Leeds, Massachusetts, which was manufacturing transfer typefaces for the graphic arts.

I contacted Bob, one of Chartpack's artists, about the possibility of having some transfer material silk-screened for me.

"What are you up to this time, Bert? It's not as simple as you think, especially where these extra-small images are concerned."

Bob's wheels started to turn as well. "First of all, we're only printing on big sheets, about 20x24 inches and that means that you have to have at least ten images on a sheet. Moreover, your little images have to be of a minimum thickness for printing as well as having enough surfaces for adherence. Thirdly, we have to determine what kind of glue to coat them with."

"We have solved bigger problems before, Bob. Remember the Kermit series? We can do it. I'll get back to you when I have it all figured out."

I really had picked myself a challenge. Because of my other work I could concentrate on this project only in the evening.

The ideas gradually emerged, but the more I thought about the process, the more complicated it became. *How many images should I use per worksheet?*

First I had to figure out the sheet size; 8½x11 would be too big and cumbersome to handle. Half that size was still too large. A sheet cut in thirds was the correct size and fit into a envelope. Now the color.

The images on the charts were printed in two colors at that time: black and red because the buoys and beacons were either red or black. The beacons' shapes are triangular for red and square for black. Red buoys, or nuns, are pointed on top and black buoys, or cans, are square on top. These shapes are important for the mariner at poor visibility when he cannot distinguish colors but recognizes the shape of the aids to navigation.

Now we need numbers and abbreviations. Also some white-outs are advisable to delete symbols for buoys that have been pulled. I must include symbols for drilling platforms, light beams for lighthouses, underwater cables and at least some symbols for international charts to complete the kit.

My head was spinning. I had to enlarge, or blow up, all these symbols twenty times their regular size and redraw them to thicken the lines for proper adhesion and printability. Then I pasted up the chart correction sheet twice its size for sharpness. This took me almost half a year.

With the paste up complete, I made a master negative and with a step-and-repeat machine exposed the image ten times on a positive film, ready for silk screening.

For the cover design I used part of a chart of coastal Maine, south of K'port, showing Cape Neddick.

When the Chart Correction Kit was ready for marketing I established the Transgraphics Division as part of Metzroth Graphics.

Thinking of Gordon, I had envisioned that individual sailors and boaters would use most of the kits but they preferred to replace their charts regularly instead of doing their corrections; an expensive choice. To my surprise, it was sailors of the U.S. Navy, Coast Guard and Merchant Marine who appreciated my work most.

The reception was immense. One Coast Guard man wrote me, "This is the best invention since the bra."

On another day I received a desperate letter from a mate on a tanker in the Persian Gulf, "We have to go around the Cape of Good Hope because of the size of our tanker and I have all the time to correct my charts. Please send me two kits."

Soon after the issue of the first edition of the Chart Correction Kit, all colors for the buoys and beacons had to be internationally changed from red and black to red and green. *A lucky break for me.* I had orders coming in daily. The chandleries asked for them by the hundreds.

But I had to rework the paste up for the third color, green, and had to do it fast to fill all these lovely orders. New negatives, new step-and-repeat, and new positives for Chartpack. Bob expedited my work so that I could ship the new regulation kits within a week.

"Why didn't you think of that earlier?" Gordon grumbled in his usual demeanor.

"You should have shown me your miserable chart correction earlier, Gordon."

"Humph, I still say we would have licked you."

"Gordon, get off the war and take your boat out."

"Can't do it anymore. My eyesight is failing me and the ticker is giving me trouble," he mentioned sadly. Here was a sailor fading into the sunset. It will hit all of us eventually.

Almut and I retired in 1989 and wanted to do some serious sailing. I sold Metzroth Graphics and gave Transgraphics to Riko because I could not handle the business from a sailboat. The kits are still selling well, not as briskly, but orders are coming in as backup to computers, especially from the Navy and the Coast Guard.

The other day, while watching TV, I saw an aircraft carrier leaving port. I turned to Almut and said, "There go my Chart Correction Kits."

"Think for yourself..." Thanks, Papa, I do.

Memorial Day 2005, Almut and Eitel

Names of the POWs buried at Camp Blanding

EPILOGUE

A person can revisit the past physically or mentally, or both. I experienced both when I first acted on my desire to see what had become of my former POW camp in Florida.

I have always referred to Camp Blanding as my alma mater, by definition the fostering mother, or institution, educating her charges. At this camp, I spent months during which I continued to mature. Gradually, the propaganda the Hitler régime had planted in my mind lost its influence. I began to think for myself, as Papa had instructed me. Thus, layer by layer of the indoctrination peeled off. While internment was not the ideal situation or the camp an ideal place to grow up, I was grateful in hindsight and considered the experience as my graduation from ignorance.

During Almut's and my visit to Camp Blanding in 1978, the camp commander found no records of the former existence of POW camps inside the large training installation. He listened with interest to my description of the POWs' facilities. On that walk, I decided to draw blueprints of my alma mater in my retirement.

In 2005, after reading *Hitler's Soldiers in the Sunshine State* by Robert D. Billinger Jr. I contacted the author. He, in turn, informed the Camp Blanding Museum curator, Major Greg Parson, of my offer to cooperate in advancing the research of the camp's history.

Major Parson invited Almut and me to retrace with him the perimeter and remaining reminders of the WWII prison camp as I had known it. Twenty-seven years had passed since our first visit to the camp. Would identification of formerly familiar sites be even more difficult at this time?

On the appointed day, the major introduced us to Bill Taylor, the Educational Guidance Counselor at the Florida Youth Challenge Academy. This school operates under the auspices of the Florida National Guard at Camp Blanding. Bill Taylor became the contact who arranged further meetings and projects.

I had finished the first edition of my book *Think for Yourself,* which included a site plan of *my* former POW camp. Before, the museum had only a sketchy drawing of the locale by a former guard. The administration realized his sketch did not correspond with the remnants of the camp. With my layout, the position of remaining concrete slabs of the bathhouses made more sense.

Accompanied by Greg Parsons and Bill Taylor, our approach to the vicinity of the prison camp led through indistinguishable areas. Only after we came to the refrigeration building could I identify some of the surroundings. The railroad tracks, which had led into the camp, were removed. The forty warehouses beside the tracks had also disappeared; only the supporting concrete pilings remained.

The physical changes clashed with my memories. I recalled my work at Warehouse 40, my crafting a fan for the sewing machine; my learning to drive the truck back and forth between the warehouses. I was touched that the refrigeration building still stood its ground and visualized our train's arrival in December of 1944 when the prisoner work detail in the building had streamed out to have a look at us.

From this point on, I could recollect some of the landscape through which we prisoners had traveled daily on the back of a truck; but only after our discovery group approached the vicinity of the original camp did I know the road.

I told Bill and Greg, that here the trucks picked up speed, rushed over the little bridge, and after they were halfway up the incline had to change gears.

"The road is in poor repair," Bill said. "Let's stop at the top of the hill. From there we'll walk farther and come to a place that may be familiar, Bert."

Arriving at a clearing, I tried to remember why this spot had meaning for me. Something was missing. The grave markers, black and white Maltese Crosses, were gone from the cemetery. Here the prisoners were buried, but where are the graves?

Bill explained that the bodies were dug up and reinterred at Fort Benning. With his students, he kept the clearing clean, had fenced the area in and placed markers on the individual sites. A wooden memorial displayed the names of the prisoners who had been buried there.

None of us spoke for a while, just observed the serenity of the place. I felt thankful to Bill for having preserved the little cemetery. A breeze wafted lightly through the foliage, whispering greetings from the past to me. *I am one of you, Kumpels. I didn't forget you.*

Among the buried was Karl Behrens whose funeral took place in December 1944 or January 1945. He had committed suicide by hanging in Clewiston, Florida. That camp was considered the worst POW camp in the U.S.A. to be in, according to the Red Cross. Florida heat, humidity and hard labor in sugar cane fields demoralized the prisoners of war.

"You know, a funny thing happened a while back," Bill said. "I had parked my truck in the back and walked with the students to weed around the grave sites. Suddenly, without our getting near the truck, the horn sounded. That happened on several occasions. But there was no reason for that. The horn had never gone off by itself in other places. Makes you think."

After this interlude, we left to have a look at the camp area. Retracing our steps, we came to an asphalt road leading straight into the woods. Aha! This is the main road leading into the camp where we had to line up to be counted in the morning.

I suddenly saw myself as a prisoner again. At the main entrance of the camp on the right, immediately by the gate, was the stockade where I had spent a week on "bread and water." Farther on, I *saw* the mess hall under which Dammann had hidden to let us know about the means of escape behind the toilet.

I visualized the administration buildings on the right side of the street and next to them the company mess halls. On the left side, I remembered the washhouses and the little walkways crossing the drainage ditch with its culverts.

Main Street of the camp as it is now.

The concrete foundations of the washroom. In the upper right corner, among the trees, a coal bin.

When, in my mind, I crossed over to the left and approached the Company 2 washhouse, the more than sixty-year-old trees and vegetation prevented me from getting closer to my barrack. I reentered reality and saw only the remaining foundation of the building. Next to it, I spotted the coal bin, which had contained the material to keep the boilers hot. Both foundation and coal bin were covered with a deep layer of foliage but the elevated rims indicated the circumference of the building and the bin. We, the four explorers, recognized also the two entrances, one to the road and the other toward the hutments. Standing at the latter entrance, I visualized again the two rows of hutments of Company 2, and a little bit deeper in the underbrush was Hut 4. At the foot of a small tree had sat the little cage for Hansi, the tailless squirrel Dammann had kept.

Back to reality. I knelt down to look at the foundation of the washhouse. Slowly removing the top foliage, I reached the cement floor. As if an electric shock went through me, I trembled when touching the very floor at the entrance through which I had entered the building years ago. Standing there, more memories came to mind. To the right of me, at the corner of the building had stood two cement washtubs, in which we did our laundry. Going to a spot in the back I said, "Here I took so many showers."

From the washhouse, I approached the area where I presumed to be the location of my hutment. Nothing remained except the huge tree next to it. No visible paths helped me to orient myself. Disappointed, we went back to the main road and followed it to the end. There we found the road, which we prisoners used to walk at night when we could not sleep because it was too hot and humid. Circle after circle we rounded inside the perimeter, always the barbed wire to our right. The guards on the towers did not bother us.

Coming to a clearing that was less overgrown, I recognized where two warehouses had stood, one containing a stage. They must have been removed later since the clearing was not as thickly overgrown. Going on, we came to the embankment created by the excavation for the soccer field. To level the grounds, prisoners transported excess soil with wheel barrows to the side of the road, thus creating the embankment. Many prisoners practiced their favorite sport, played intramural games or against the Navy team on that field.

While Major Parsons served in Afghanistan in 2005, the camp commander invited me to address visitors to Camp Blanding and town's people on Memorial Day. Along with another speaker, Mr. Kan from Fort Lauderdale, we recounted to the audience our connections to the camp and its soldiers. A liberating unit, which had trained at Camp Blanding, freed Mr. Kan from a concentration camp near Magdeburg, Germany..

After the moving ceremony, we visited the museum and showed Eitel, who had flown in from Connecticut, the diorama Bill Taylor and his students created. They followed my plans and stories with amazing accuracy, down to the POWs, jail, and watchtowers.

I have gone back to Camp Blanding several times and always found more reminders of my time there. Although the POW camp is already history, it will always be part of me.

CPSIA information can be obtained
at www.ICGtesting.com
Printed in the USA
FFOW01n1952071114
8580FF